36 Stratagems for Investors

Timeless Financial Wisdom from a Chinese Classic

36 Stratagems for Investors

Timeless Financial Wisdom from a Chinese Classic

汇 丰 ◆ 晋 信

HSBC Jintrust Fund Management

Translated by
Celine Tng

WILEY

John Wiley & Sons (Asia) Pte. Ltd.

Other Wiley Editorial Offices

John Wiley & Sons, 111 River Street, Hoboken, NJ 07030, USA

John Wiley & Sons, The Atrium, Southern Gate, Chichester, West Sussex, P019 8SQ,
United Kingdom

John Wiley & Sons (Canada) Ltd., 5353 Dundas Street West, Suite 400, Toronto, Ontario, M9B
6HB, Canada

John Wiley & Sons Australia Ltd, 42 McDougall Street, Milton, Queensland 4064, Australia

Wiley-VCH, Boschstrasse 12, D-69469 Weinheim, Germany

Library of Congress Cataloging-in-Publication Data:

ISBN 978-0-470-82433-7

The HSBC logo is a registered trademark of the HSBC Group. HSBC Jintrust is duly authorized
to use the trademark.

Typeset in 11.5/14pt Bembo by Aptara Inc., New Delhi, India
Printed in Singapore by Saik Wah Press Pte. Ltd.

10 9 8 7 6 5 4 3 2 1

Contents

v

Foreword

Within two years of its inception, HSBC Jintrust published two books. The first was *Honglou Fortune—Wealth for Generations*. And this is the second, *36 Stratagems for Investors—Timeless Financial Wisdom from A Chinese Classic*. In both instances, we use ancient Chinese Classics as reference points largely because traditional Chinese culture has made its influence felt far and wide, and is therefore able to trigger a fair degree of resonance. Another reason is that scholars from the ancient times have much to offer in terms of their intellectual discourse and wisdom, even to people in the modern day and age. Their thoughts and teachings could very well bring us enlightenment and solutions to many of the problems that we often struggle to come to grips with.

The 36 Stratagems are a collection of the military tactics and strategies employed in ancient China. Many of the terms coined for the stratagems have evolved into popular proverbs. More often than not, reverse psychology and divergent thinking are tactics used to take the enemy by surprise. In our attempt to incorporate such tactical moves into fund investment, we discover they make the key rationales for fund investment much easier to comprehend and relate to.

As Confucius was recorded as saying in *Yi Zhuan*, or the *Commentary on the Book of Change* (also known as *I-Ching*), a feasible plot must be one that the masses can partake in. Hence, military generals and commanders do not have exclusive rights over the use of strategies. Everyone should be able to adopt the 36 Stratagems for problem solving. This book uses each of the 36 Stratagems to guide investors on how to identify and pick a trustworthy fund company as well as a suitable fund product, how to earn higher returns and avoid unnecessary losses, as well as how to avoid all sorts of common mistakes.

Generally speaking, in an emerging market, investors may invest in funds in the same way as they think and do in stocks. As a result, these investors may develop many habitual biases and misconceptions. However, as the market gradually matures and investors begin to choose to move collectively in the same direction, it will become a force to be reckoned with, to the extent of effecting a major market differentiation and restructuring exercise. I believe there will come a time when fund companies undergo further vertical segmentation to increase their focus on niche investment areas. Consequently, investors will cease to rely solely on their impressions of fund companies to make their choices. Instead, they will pay greater attention to a series of composite benchmarks, consisting of performance results, services, level of professionalism, and company image. Investors will also cease to pick fund products purely for short-term rate of return. Instead, they will build a portfolio of products strategically tailored to their personal as well as families' needs.

Of course, I hope growing acceptance of these two books will help bring about greater transparency and progress to the fund industry. We hope to work hand in hand with the industry to realize rational fund investing. To use Hollywood as an analogy, Tinsel Town is not merely a processing plant for movie productions. It has produced numerous derivative products that have become trailblazers and trendsetters in more ways than one to effect changes in people's lifestyles and values. I believe fund investing is not so imposing and daunting that only a handful of people are able to comprehend it. By incorporating it into our culture, it will be transformed from a series of boring numbers into a lifelong lifestyle concept.

I would like to extend my heartfelt thanks to Ms. Rena He Hanxi and her team for their top-notch work and astuteness in the market, their efforts in culling and compiling copious amount of market case studies and materials, as well as their judicious professional attitude and insurmountable passion in writing this book. I believe many of the examples and thoughts cited in the book will remain useful and valuable references even after years when the market has undergone a sea of changes.

I sincerely hope that every reader and investor will stand to gain from this little book.

Steve Lee
CEO
HSBC Jintrust Fund Management

Stratagem 1

Fool the Emperor to Cross the Sea (瞒天过海)

See Through All Guises for Calculated Returns

Origin of the Stratagem

Emperor Tang Taizong, the second emperor of the Tang Dynasty, who ruled from 626 AD to 649 AD, was said to have once led 300,000 soldiers from Changan to Liaodong. When the troops arrived at a beach, Emperor Tang Taizong looked troubled as he scanned the cold and choppy waters. Sensing his anxiety, General Xue Rengui invited the emperor to join him and his soldiers in a tent for some food and wine.

Music filled the air. All the merrymaking soon made the emperor relax and forget his worries. However, the respite was cut short by the sound of abrupt and thunderous waves. Worried, the emperor took a cautious peek out of the tent. To his surprise, his war vessels had set off without his knowledge, and were almost reaching the opposite shore of the sea. This tactic employed by General Xue Rengui is still used by the military today, as they carry out stealth missions.

New Spin on Funds

US$1 funds and the truth about net asset value
Performance indicators
Do your math

US$1 funds and the truth about net asset value

Investors love "US$1 funds," as the very claim of US$1 net asset value (NAV) seems such a bargain, compared with a US$2 net asset value. In fact, the net asset value alone does not tell us anything. It is also a fallacy to judge a fund's performance based on its net asset value. More critically, we should take into consideration the history of the fund, the potential dividend payouts, how the fund compares with the performance of similar funds in the market, and so on. Someone may say: "This fund has a net asset value of just US$1 right now. You should buy it!" That should raise the red flag. Do not be fooled.

Truth be told, a "US$1 fund" does not enjoy any advantage over other funds in terms of its growth potential, except for the fact that a US$1 fund makes returns easy to calculate and follow. Even a spinoff will not affect the asset size of a "US$1 fund." The only change in the event of a spinoff is an increase in its holdings, which offers a fair amount of flexibility if you decide to buy back or swap your shares.

Performance indicators

A bias toward "low net-asset-value funds" is not encouraged. If you are not convinced, the following arguments may well change your mind. Smart fund investors always do their homework with regard to how fund investment returns are calculated, the fund's net asset value per share, as well as the correlation between accumulative net asset value and dividends.

Net asset value per share, accumulative net asset value, and dividends are direct indices of a fund's investment returns. Net asset value per share refers to the actual value of a single unit at a certain point in time. It is a key index to measure how well or how badly a fund is managed. It is also an indication of the bidding and buyback (trading) price of a unit of fund. The prices do not factor in dividends which reflect the profitability of a fund. It shows the fund's actual earning power.

Accumulative net asset value is the total sum of the latest net asset value and accumulated dividends, which reflects the accumulated net income of the fund since its inception. Accumulative net value also tells us about a fund's dividend performance. Hence, accumulative net asset value is more important than the latest net asset value or dividend as an indicator for an investor to measure investment returns. Accumulative net asset value captures more directly and broadly the performance of the fund in operation. Higher accumulative net asset value generally means the fund is faring better than before.

Dividends refer to cash payouts or dividend reinvestment awarded to fund shareholders for profit made.

Do your math

Always bear in mind two considerations in calculating the rate of return from a fund. An investment period promising no dividend clearly means that the overall rate of return is the same as the growth rate of net asset value per share within a certain period (without taking into account fees and charges). For example, an open-end fund valued at US$1 at the end of last year and US$1.06 at the end of this year will yield an overall rate of return of 6 percent this year. The method used to calculate this is: (US$1.06 − 1) ÷ 1 = 6 percent. Multiply your total investment sum by 6 percent, and you will find out your returns for the entire period.

What if there is a dividend payout? You will see net asset value per share taking a dip after the payout. Let's say net asset value per share stands at $1.06 before the payout, and dividend per share comes up to $0.05. Net asset value per share after the payout will drop to $1.01. In this case, you have to factor in the impact of the dividend on net asset value when calculating the overall return on investment. If you have difficulty tallying up the numbers yourself, simply go to MorningStar Fund QuickRank to check out the indices called "Total Return Percentage." Having said that, investors should bear in mind that MorningStar's method of calculation for the rate of return is based on the assumption that dividends are reinvested. Hence, if you opt for cash payouts, and invest the dividends or spend the money elsewhere, your actual income will be somewhat different from the calculated rate of return.

An investor should note that net asset value per share affects only the size of your holdings, not your future returns on investment. Let's say there are two funds, called Fund A and Fund B, with a net asset value of $1 and $2 respectively. You invest $20,000 in each fund, which gives you 20,000 shares in Fund A and 10,000 shares in Fund B. Assuming the net asset values of both funds surge 20 percent after three months (with no dividend payout during this period), the net asset value of Fund A and Fund B will now stand at US$1.20 and US$2.40 respectively. Can you tell what the current market value of the fund is? Check out the answer below.

Market value of Fund A   US$1.20 × 20,000 = US$24,000
Market value of Fund B   US$2.40 × 10,000 = US$24,000

You will discover that the returns from both funds are the same. The net asset value at the time of purchase makes no difference at all.

Therefore, there is no such thing as a cheaper or more expensive fund. Whether or not a fund is worth investing in depends on its future earning power. When we talk about a fund having high accumulative net asset value, we are referring to the caliber and capability of its managers, and the fund's resilience in weathering different market conditions in the past. That earns the fund greater trust with investors. The level at which the net asset value is at has no direct impact on the future value of the fund either.

A share price gets its boost from a listed company's prospective ability to create greater profit. Once the company's profitability lags behind the rate at which the share price is rising, the share price inevitably falters. A share price is prone to adjust downward once it scales to a certain height. A fund invests in myriad stocks that are considered a basket of good "eggs." Periodically, the fund manager will remove "rotten eggs" from the lot, and replace them with "good ones." Therefore, a fund has to adopt a sound strategy in picking stocks, and make appropriate adjustments in the investment portfolio to propel its net asset value higher.

Stratagem 2

Besiege Wei to Rescue Zhao (围魏救赵)

Take Advantage of Fund Switching

Origin of the Stratagem

In 354 BC, when King Weihui sent General Pang Juan to attack the Zhao State's capital of Handan, the king of Zhao immediately sought help from King Qi Weiwang of the Qi State. Tasked with the defense mission, military advisor Sun Bin offered his strategy to General Tian Ji who was commanding the Qi troops: "Do not get into a mindless fistfight. Resolve the problem without getting into a struggle. Find out their weaknesses to gain the upper hand without having to resort to violence. The Wei troops are out in full force. If we attack them head-on, Pang Juan is bound to beat a retreat. He will lose his stranglehold on Handan. We shall ambush him midway and defeat his troops."

Tian Ji carried out the mission as planned. True to Sun Bin's predictions, the Wei troops left Handan and were ambushed by the Qi army at Guiling. Exhausted after a long march and fight, the Wei army surrendered. The Qi State emerged on top by coming to the rescue of the Zhao State.

New Spin on Funds

Fund swap as a way out
- The less costly route
- Swap medium- and high-risk funds for low-risk funds
- Change tack according to market conditions
- The difference in risk endurance

Fund swap as a way out

Stock markets are volatile and unpredictable. Fund investors will inevitably get caught when the markets trend downward. Whether or not to redeem funds becomes a burning issue. Pulling out of one may spell losses, while staying put means having to bear with the pain of a downward spiral in net asset value.

Learning to adopt the stratagem as illustrated in the classic story "besiege Wei to save Zhao" may well save you the angst. Shift your attention away from the glare of the "bears" that are out in full force by making good and flexible use of fund companies' swap services. Convert a share-based fund into a currency fund belonging to the same company at an appropriate time to protect future earnings, and prevent losses. Reconvert it into a share-based fund only when the stock markets are back in favor. By turning a share-based into a currency fund, or by buying a currency fund, you are making good use of your investment in a share-based fund. It is a tactic worth borrowing from the war strategy used by the Qi army to save Zhao.

The less costly route. Swapping funds is a key transaction method used in overseas markets. In China, several fund companies have started to do the same. A fund swap refers to an investor's request for a fund manager to diversify all or part of his or her holdings in a fund into another or other funds. A fund swap produces the same result as the redemption or re-subscription of a fund, but the inner workings of the two are as different as chalk and cheese. A fund swap costs less transaction time and money than redemption and re-subscription. The transaction of a fund swap takes three to five working days, while redemption and re-subscription requires five to seven working days. The monetary costs of a fund swap are divided into three components, namely the redemption fee for the exiting fund, the differential in subscription fees between the exiting fund and replacement fund, and the fund swap fee which is usually set at zero. The total rate charges of these fees are generally lower than the redemption rate and re-subscription rate.

A fund swap has to take place at the right place and the right time to produce the desired investment effect, just as Tian Ji timed his move to besiege the strongholds of the Wei State to trap Pang Juan into submission.

Swap medium- and high-risk funds for low-risk funds. Swapping a low-risk currency fund with a high-risk share-based fund is an example of the most effective fund swap. Swapping funds with similar risk returns is only recommended if there is a huge gap in performance between the fund you wish to exit from and the one you wish to get into. Oftentimes, such a gap is inherent in the management of the fund.

Change tack according to market conditions. You can discern signs of whether a stock market is doing well or poorly by making a meticulous study of macro trends. If the market is mired by bears, convert share-based funds into bond or currency funds to avoid losses from shrinking net asset value. When the stock market is flying high, trade bond and currency funds for share-based funds to enjoy more lucrative long-term investment returns.

The difference in risk endurance. Age may make an impact on a person's income. Older folks are likely to face more health issues, which will affect their work ability. That may lead to a drop in income level. Any investor in such a dilemma should trade share-based funds for bonds or currency bonds to raise the safety net of an investment portfolio. At the other end of the spectrum are the individuals enjoying job promotions, incremental increases in their salaries, and other improved conditions. As these people are able to endure risk better, they should, as investors, convert bonds or currency bonds into share-based funds to beef up their investment portfolio returns.

Practical tips

How best to convert funds?

1. T + 0 for greater profit
Convert a currency fund into a share-based fund on T day, according to the net asset value of the currency fund quoted that day. T day refers to the trade date. This enables the investor to lock in profits from the currency fund at the same time.

2. Make use of the time difference and overlap in time
In general, banks take five to seven working days to complete the transaction for the redemption of a share-based fund, a bond fund, or a composite fund. However, you can convert any type of fund into currency funds in just two days, and complete the redemption and transaction process in one to three working days. Hence, learn to capitalize on the gaps between the maturity dates of different types of funds, and the mechanism for fund conversion provided by fund management companies. Convert all types of funds to currency funds before redemption. This speeds up transactions, and allows you to reap several more days of returns from currency funds.

Stratagem 3

Kill with a Borrowed Sword (借刀杀人)

Gain Full Market Exposure in One Go

Origin of the Stratagem

Before his attack on the Wei State during the Spring-Autumn Period from 800 BC to 300 BC, Zheng Huangong got a hold of the names of Wei's ministers and generals. He then announced that after he had defeated Wei, he would make them lords and dukes, and let them share the Wei territory. Zheng Huangong put the names in an urn at an altar that he had set up in the country, and swore to deliver on his promise.

The king of Wei was furious when he got wind of the news, and gave orders for all his great ministers and generals to be sent to the guillotine. In one fell swoop, the Zheng State had destroyed the Wei State.

New Spin on Funds

Leverage through a third party
- Amass huge capital gains through funds
- Explore unfamiliar territories

Financial management is a buzzword these days. With a constant stream of new products coming into the marketplace every day, the average investor can't help but feel bombarded and perplexed. Worst of all, individual investors often do not qualify for some of these products, or find many of the products too difficult to comprehend. So, how should one invest? You may want to consider taking a leaf out of the "killing with a borrowed sword" stratagem. Fear not, there is no blood and gore involved. It simply means riding on the strength of a third party to realize one's financial goals. In other words, use the power of funds as a leveraging tool to boost your profit.

Leverage through a third party

The Chinese are fond of government bonds, but few know of the more lucrative, similar products out there that they may qualify for. For example, individual investors cannot invest in the banking bond market and corporate bonds due to restricted retail sales, insufficient individual investor demand, and so forth. However, purchases of bonds such as central bank treasury bills and corporate bonds can be made indirectly through the acquisition of bond funds.

Some individual investors also bemoan lost opportunities in the stock markets. In general, listed companies have to suspend stock trading for a period before announcing any shareholding changes or other major events, and their share prices tend to soar when they resume trading. With the market rife with talk about shareholding changes, and public notices being hoisted, investors often can anticipate a surge in company stock prices, but they are not able to cash in on the profits when trading activity is suspended. One way to get around this is to purchase funds that are heavily weighted in those listed companies suspended from trading. You can expect share prices to rally right after the suspension is lifted, giving the funds' net asset value a real boost.

Amass huge capital gains through funds. Funds are great investment tools for creating and amassing capital gains on a grand scale, while just putting money with every other stock in the stock market will not enable you to build an investment portfolio. Buying a RMB1,000 fund is as good as acquiring 20 to 30 stocks to form a portfolio of investments that spread out the risk.

Furthermore, large capital gains amassed through funds sharpen an investor's competitive edge. When it comes to securing new shares, an individual investor is nowhere near an institutional investor in terms of accessibility to participation channels, professional experience, and the size of working capital. As a result, individual investors usually end up playing second fiddle to institutional investors in the queue for new shares. Since that is the case, there is no real need for individual investors to get so actively involved. Let funds do the job for you more effectively, as the example below shows.

Most funds mobilize large pools of capital online (even though offline channels are also used) to subscribe to new shares, and bolster the success rate in application and subscription. There are even bond funds created for that sole purpose. For instance, on September 17, 2007, frozen capital for online and offline subscription of China Construction Bank Corporation Limited Company shares totaled RMB2.26 trillion (US$331 billion). Final offline sales accounted for 2.836 percent, and final lots drawn online to be offered shares made up 2.468 percent. Evidently, individuals who applied online received fewer shares than funds that applied offline for the share offering. Funds had the advantage of being able to apply online and offline simultaneously. China Construction Bank set its offer price at RMB6.45 (US$0.939). As of October 30, 2007, the bank's share price stood at RMB10.86 (US$1.58). Have we managed to convince you now that it is much easier to secure new shares through funds?

Explore unfamiliar territories. Right certification, convertible bonds, index-futures pricing... They belong to an endless string of new terms that investors have to grapple with. It can be time-consuming and draining to try to figure out all the different terms and types of products. This is where funds can provide the best solutions. Invest in funds and leave the expert fund managers to worry about these complex issues. Make the fund manager with the "three highs" (high culture, high education, and high income) work for you. You can also purchase the QDII products that fund companies have launched to invest in various markets abroad, and reap the benefits of spreading out your investment and risk (refer to Stratagems 35 and 36, where QDII is covered in greater detail).

Stratagem 4

Bide Your Time to Wear Down the Enemy (以逸待劳)

Take a Long-Term View

Origin of the Stratagem

Toward the end of the Warring States Period (453 BC–221 BC), the Qin State decided to call upon retired General Wang Jian to lead a 600,000-strong army to mount an attack against the Chu State. Just as they were closing in on the Chu State, the latter launched a massive counterattack. General Wang Jian decided not to respond in kind. Instead, he focused on fixing the moat, and appeared to be taking a defensive stance, when in fact he was discreetly telling his troops to conserve their energy.

A year later, the Chu army soldiers relaxed their guard, and began to lose their fighting spirit. Convinced that the Qin troops were indeed taking a defensive stance, the Chu soldiers backed east. Wang Jian immediately pounced on the opportunity to take them by surprise. The Qin troops went on a rampage, and killed every Chu soldier in their way. The Qin soldiers were on an unbeatable path. Eventually, in 223 BC, the Qin State swallowed the Chu State.

New Spin on Funds

To hold or let go
• The rationale

To hold or let go

Market volatility often causes the net asset value of share-based funds to gyrate. No doubt, this can be a huge test of a fund investor's psychological ability to take the heat. In the face of market turbulence and a continuous upswing in the indices, many fund investors feel stuck as they are torn between whether to hold on to a fund or let it go.

To an investor hoping to ride on the back of China's bull markets, withdrawing from a fund without more attractive alternative investment avenues to fall back on is a risk. It entails a reinvestment risk, or the risk of missing out on the fund's future returns. Even reinvesting in a bull market involves high stakes. Can you find better investment tools than the fund you are thinking of pulling out of? A fund that reaps satisfactory returns but does not look particularly rosy in its future prospects may trigger your desire for a fund swap. It is indeed advisable to make a redemption and park your money in another fund at this point in time. There is no need to pull out of the fund completely to steer clear of the risks in a turbulent market. Besides, you may decide to reinvest in the same fund after the market gloom has blown over.

The rationale. The reasons are easy to understand. The rates of the handling fees for redemption and reinvestment are high. Together, they add up to 2 percent. A fund investor who has just entered the fray may find himself or herself left with fairly meager returns after the handling fees are deducted.

Fear and greed frequently drive investors to buy at the highest level and sell at the lowest level of different wave bands. Market plunges often make investors cry foul and abandon ship prematurely for fear of suffering losses. Similarly, many investors strike it rich overnight in red-hot markets, and greed may cause them to go after bigger gains even in the face of exceedingly high risks. Chasing the highs and eliminating the lows are parts of the human makeup, and are foibles that few people can control. When it comes to the crunch, people rarely sell high and buy low.

Tracking the wave bands of stock trading is no walk in the park. Just biding one's time is probably the simplest and most effective investment approach in dealing with uncertain situations. This is proven in statistical studies. Assuming you had invested in Stock A at the beginning of a year within the period between 1991 and 2007, the probability of a negative investment return after one year would be 41.18 percent. After three years, it would be 33.33 percent. After six years, it would sink to 8.33 percent. After nine years the probability of negative investment return would drop to zero, guaranteeing no loss of income.

The history of fund development in China is proof that funds are effective instruments of long-term finance management. From 1998 to 2006, the average annual rate of investment return of share-based funds or composite funds stood at 22.48 percent. The year 1998 saw the inception of the first batch of close-end funds, namely Fund Kaiyuan, Fund Jintai, Fund Xinghua, Fund Anxin, and Fund Yuyang. From then until September 30, 2007, they chalked up a net average accumulative growth of 535.37 percent.

Hence, regardless of the ups and downs in the market cycle, maintain a positive focus as long as the bulls are holding the fort in the market over the long run. That does not mean you should adopt a passive attitude of doing nothing. It is still essential to regularly appraise the funds that you hold. This includes checks on the investment philosophies, strategies, changes in fund managers, fund performance, risk rankings, developmental changes over the different periods, comparative average rate of return between the funds and the market, comparative rankings in risk levels, changes in dividend plans, fund holdings, and heavyweights holdings.

Stratagem 5

Loot a Burning House (趁火打劫)

Never Attempt to Get Away with a Steal

Origin of the Stratagem

The Chinese proverb "get away with a steal" originally means to rob someone of his or her property when a house is on fire. To put the stratagem in a military context, it means to take advantage of a troubled situation in the enemy's camp, and deal it a double whammy.

During the Spring-Autumn Period which lasted from 800 BC to 300 BC, the Wu State and the Yue State were fighting constantly to dominate each other. The Yue State was ultimately no match for the Wu State, so it crumbled. King Gou Jian of the Yue State was, however, determined to make a comeback. On the surface, he appeared subservient to win the trust of King Fu Chai of the

21

Wu State, and was finally released, and allowed to return to the Yue State.

Meanwhile, victory had made Fu Chai rest on his laurels. Not only had he grown complacent, but also arrogant and cruel. He turned a deaf ear to sound advice, preferring the counsel of corrupt officials. In 473 BC, poor crop harvests stirred up great dissatisfaction among the Yue people. When Fu Chai headed up north to meet with Central Plains clan tribes in Huangchi to forge alliances, Gou Jian seized the opportunity to attack the Wu State. With no one holding the fort in the kingdom, the Wu State quickly crumbled under the Yue State's attack. Gou Jian's victory is a classic example of the military tactic of getting away with a steal.

New Spin on Funds

"Stock up" when net asset value heads south
Covet market darlings, switch product types regularly
Aim long, not short

Most investors embrace the concept of "opportunism" and put the notion "get away with a steal" to work even in their fund investment. Below are some examples.

"Stock up" when net asset value heads south

Some fund investors believe that when the net asset value in a fund takes a hit, it is time to fish for more bargains. This is fundamentally the concept of a low-cost strategy at work, but it can be fallible rather than the best investment approach to take at times. The price level of a fund at the time of purchase is beside the point.

The keys lie in:

- The difference in price between the future net asset value and the net asset value at the time of purchase. This is referred to as the "potential gains" of a fund.
- The difference in ratio between the future net asset value and the net asset value at the time of purchase. This is also known as the "rate of net asset value growth."

Covet market darlings, switch product types regularly

In 2006, the China A-share market recorded the world's highest market increases, and the rate of return for share-based funds surpassed 100 percent. The phenomena lured droves of investors who had never before dabbled in stocks to become fund investors. However, the shareholding distribution and allocation reform soon brought an end to the overall surge in the broader market. Share prices begun to subside, and sector buying became a holding pattern. Heavyweights and topical market news set the tone of market direction. Consequently, value-investment concept-driven funds lagged behind share index growth.

At the beginning of 2007, low-priced small-cap stocks became the darlings of the markets. News and speculation such as backdoor listings, restructuring, and bulk orders all catapulted prices of these stocks to dizzying heights. The performance of value-based investment funds paled in comparison. The first quarter of 2007 saw only 14 funds surpass the SSE 300 Index in performance, thus sparking an exodus of investors from funds to direct investment in stocks.

Aim long, not short

"Getting away with a steal" is the worst enemy of any fund investor in search of long-term gains. Investors often put such great store in maximizing short-terms gains that they tend to overlook their long-range goals and the equally viable average rate of return of most funds in the long term. Short-term profitability is no definitive measure of long-term gains. From 2002 to 2008, different funds

Table 5.1 2002–08 rate of return of top open-end funds

2002	Huaxia Growth Fund	−3.09%
2003	Boshi Value Growth Fund	34.39%
2004	ABN AMRO Teda Fund	17.06%
2005	GF Stable Growth Fund	16.96%
2006	Jingshun Great Wall Domestic Demand Growth Fund	182.22%
2007	China AMC Large-Cap Select Fund	226.24%
2008	BOCOM Schroders Enhanced Yield Bond Fund	13.05%

took the top spot on the profitability charts (see Table 5.1). Some funds shot to the top one year and sank to the bottom of the list the next. Frequent subscription and redemption of funds is often responsible for spiraling costs that erode investors' long-term gains.

Funds are products that are suited for long-term investment. Therefore, forget about making away with a steal where funds are concerned. The plan will only backfire. The majority of funds will only yield market average profit in the long run. Despite that, there are two ways to reap more than just the market average rate of return.

First, identify funds or fund companies with strong management capabilities, and engage them over a long period. Second, keep the transaction costs as low as possible, and extend your holding periods to offset the adverse impact of short- to medium-term fluctuations and transaction costs, as well as to maximize your level of profitability.

Stratagem 6

Clamor in the East and Attack the West (声东击西)

Arbitrage Opportunities in Fund Investing

Origin of the Stratagem

"Clamor in the east and attack the west" describes a person making a pretense of planning to attack a territory to cover up his or her intention to invade another. It is a stratagem of leaving false tracks, creating false impressions, and sending mixed signals to confuse an adversary into making the wrong judgments, before killing them off.

In the Eastern Han Period, Ban Chao was sent to the Western Region to annex the Shache State ruled by the Xiongnu barbarians. The Shache State quickly sought help from the Guizi State, and the latter responded by commanding 50,000 soldiers to rescue the

Shache State. Armed with only a 25,000-strong force, Ban Chao knew he was no match for Guizi, and only a brilliant battle plan would save the day.

At dusk, he ordered his troops to beat a retreat, and make a show of chaos which included turning some prisoners loose. As these prisoners of war believed they were genuinely free at last, they returned to inform Guizi of the chaos that had broken out in Ban Chao's camp. Guizi immediately ordered his soldiers to go after the enemies. In truth, Ban Chao had only retreated 5 km., with his troops hiding in ambush. Impatient to make his conquest, the King of Guizi led his soldiers in hot pursuit of the enemies who he believed were on the run. The King of Guizi did not even realize that he had actually crossed their path and missed them. Ban Chao promptly commanded his men to make a quick charge for the Shache State. Taken by surprise, the Shache State did not have much of a chance to put up a fight before it fell.

New Spin on Funds

Alternative funds
- Listed open-end funds
- Exchange-traded funds

Alternative funds

Since funds are medium- to long-term investment products, they are always best to hold on to for stability. There are also the alternative funds that can be transacted in two different markets. That means an investor can purchase funds in one market to sell them in another, or offload funds in one market with the purpose of acquiring them in the other. By buying and selling on both ends, the investor realizes a profit with no risk incurred.

Exchange-traded funds (ETFs) and listed open-end funds (LOFs) are the alternative funds available in the market. ETFs are, in fact, a unique brand of index-linked funds. Investors are able to buy and sell ETF holdings in the secondary markets, apply for subscription with the fund management companies, and redeem ETF holdings from the primary markets. Albeit, this comes with conditions attached including subscription and redemption must take the form of an exchange of either a basket of shares (sometimes a small amount of cash) for a shareholding of funds, or vice versa. There are currently five ETF products listed on the SSE 50 Index, the SSE 180 Index, the SSE SME Board Index, the SSE Dividend Index, and the SSZE 100 Index. LOFs have simpler features and are fairly similar to open-end funds as they are either index-linked or share-based funds, with the added capability to engage in exchange trading. Twenty-two LOFs are currently trading in the market, including China Southern's allocation funds and Boshi's theme funds.

ETFs and LOFs are priced according to the net asset value of funds in subscription and redemption in the primary markets, and follow the transaction prices when trading at exchanges. Therefore, a widening gap between the net asset value of a fund and the transaction price presents the best opportunity to lock in profits.

Listed open-end funds. It is relatively easy to take profit in LOFs as it involves only fund transactions. For example, with the net asset value of an LOF per unit standing at US$1.20, and the exchange market value at US$1.10, an investor can acquire fund holdings from the exchange, and apply for custodianship, then redeem those holdings at the primary market two days later. If the net asset value of the fund remains unchanged, it means a US$0.10 profit in hand.

Obviously, this is an extreme example. An investor cashing in profits will undoubtedly have to take into consideration the costs of transaction, including subscription fees of 1 percent to 1.5 percent, redemption fees of approximately 0.5 percent, LOF secondary market trading fees of roughly 0.2 percent on a single end, and custodial fees of about 2 percent. Apart from all these direct charges, there is also the time cost. Locking in LOF profits takes at least three days, and there is a huge risk in trying to predict how prices or the net asset value of the fund will change in three days. If the price differential disappears altogether or turns negative, the investor will suffer a loss instead. Hence, taking LOF profits may seem pedestrian and a fair game for everyone, but in reality it is not easy to execute successfully.

Exchange-traded funds. By comparison, there are many more opportunities to take profits in ETFs, and this can be done at the snap of a finger:

- **Trade-driven arbitrage**
  If the net asset value of an ETF per unit supersedes its exchange market price, an investor should acquire fund holdings from the exchange, then buy back in the primary market a basket of shares before selling them. The reverse is recommended if the ETF's market price is higher than its net asset value per unit. In other words, an investor can purchase a basket of shares, then use it to subscribe to fund holdings in the primary market before selling the ETF holdings in the secondary market.
- **Event-driven arbitrage**
  This is a fairly simple profit-taking operation. For example, an index constituent stock may be suspended from trading due to shareholding changes, or a major restructuring program, or some other positive events. The stock may not be available in the secondary market, but it is still possible to invest in it by snapping up ETFs in the same market. Then you make your redemption, convert them into a basket of shares in the primary market, and sell the other index constituent stocks in the secondary market, keeping what you are truly after—the shares that are suspended from trading.

With the introduction of index futures, ETFs can be treated as a form of cash commodity assets. When differentials in the prices of futures and cash commodities emerge, it is a good time to lock in profits in index futures.

However, ETFs are more the game of big corporate investors who are able to fork out enormous sums of money to take huge profits. The rule of the game is such that the subscription of a basket of shares for ETFs must hit at least RMB1 million (US$143,000) and it is an arbitrage process involving numerous custodial transactions. The trading distribution and ratio of the basket of shares can also be rather complicated, and operable only on specific ETF arbitrage transaction systems.

Leveraging different markets for arbitrage trading to make the most short-term gains in funds sounds really attractive, but it is not always accessible to everyone.

Practical tips

Why are ETFs so popular?

1. Advantages of index-based investments
- Index-based investments ensure an even spread and lower the risk.
- A single ETF transaction enables the buying and selling of many stocks.
- There is transparency as the performance of funds moves in tandem with the direction of the indices. When an index falls, funds fall. When an index rises, funds rise.

2. Advantages of exchange-linked transactions
- Transactions are straightforward and flexible:

  a. Transaction prices can be locked in immediately.
  b. Capital is used more effectively.
  c. It provides convenience in trading. Buying and selling can occur within the same trading day.

- Transactions made can be converted to cash easily.

3. Unique advantages of ETFs
- Low management and trading costs.
- Prices are traded and kept at reasonable levels.
- Potential to expand the markets, boost share trading volumes, and raise the level of efficiency of market operations.

Why are LOFs out of favor?

1. Fuzzy investment structure
- LOFs are limited to currently listed open-end funds that may be linked to an index or an exchange. They lack a clear structure.
- There is poor transparency as LOF products consist of a portfolio of funds that report performance only on a quarterly basis. Hence, investors are unable to see or track the performance of the funds very well.

2. Lackluster exchange-based trading
- It offers merely another platform for selling and buying funds.
- There are delays in trading applications and processing of custodial changes for funds after redemption.

3. Few unique advantages
- Compared to existing ETFs, LOFs lack innovative products.
- LOFs only feature simple functional add-ons from open-end funds to existing close-end funds.
- Cash transactions increase the operating costs of funds, while chronic delays in effecting custodial changes blunt the edge for profit-making.

Stratagem 7

Create Something from Nothing
(无中生有)

Details, Details, Details!

Origin of the Stratagem

During the Anshi Rebellion in 755 AD in the Tang Dynasty, Tang General Zhang Xun led approximately 3,000 men to defend Yongqiu against An Lushan's 40,000-strong army led by General Ling Huchao. The odds were stacked against Zhang Xun and his troops as they faced a more formidable adversary and struggled with a depleting supply of arrows.

Zhang Xun suddenly had a thought. He ordered his men to create thousands of straw men dressed up in black to be lowered slowly down the fortress. In the dark of the night, Ling Huchao thought Zhang Xun had launched a sneak attack, and ordered his men to fire off a quick succession of arrows. Ten thousand arrows fell right into Zhang Xun's hands. The next morning, Ling Huchao was shattered when he realized he had walked right into the enemy's trap.

When Zhang Xun repeated the motion of lowering straw men down his fortress the second night, Ling Huchao and his men laughed out loud. Little did they realize that 500 of Zhang Xun's warriors had used the night darkness as a camouflage to slip down the fortress and sneak up on them. Taken off-guard, Ling Huchao and his men took a beating before they could make their escape.

New Spin on Funds

Subscribe early for a better head start
Opt for back-end fee payment
Reinvest dividends for better interest
Purchase online to save time and energy

The Chinese proverb "to create something from nothing" is commonly used these days to mean the fabrication of tales and lies. In the art of war where the phrase originates, it refers to the creation of a mock situation that quickly transcends into a real event, or turning an initial act of deception into something real to confuse and defeat one's foe. The key is to produce something out of nothing. We, too, can achieve the same effect and boost our investment returns in ways that we least expect if we pay attention to a few details.

Subscribe early for a better head start

A fund charges different rates for fees at its initial subscription launch, and after the closed period when it reopens for application. Subscription fees are always lower than application fees by approximately 0.3 of a percentage point. If saving on fees is key, then it is advisable to subscribe to a fund that you want at the launch rather than wait till later. Besides, the interest yields from capital growth during the subscription period will be calculated based on the savings interest rate of financial industry peers. It stands at 0.99 percent at the time of writing, while banks hand out an after-tax savings interest rate of 0.7695 percent. When the fund is officially set up, part of the interest rate earned will be injected into the client's fund holdings, and exempt from the 5 percent personal income tax. So be an early subscriber to reap advance profit, and put every cent to good use.

Opt for back-end fee payment

Front-end and back-end are the two models of fee charges in the purchase of funds. When an open-end fund requires you to pay the subscription or the application fees upfront, these are called front-end charges. The purchase comes with no handling charges. The fees you pay at a later stage in your application to redeem your fund holdings are called back-end charges. Under the model of the back-end fees, the subscription fees are not deducted at the point of subscription. Your entire investment is converted into fund holdings so that every cent is immediately turned into a money-making machine. Back-end charges generally tend to decrease over an extended period in fund holdings, and after a given time frame (normally four to five years), the application charges are usually waived so the cost of the fund purchase is as good as zero.

Reinvest dividends for better interest

Cash dividend and dividend reinvestment are two types of dividends that fund investors can opt for. Dividend reinvestment does not incur any application charges. Part of the dividend is converted into fund holdings based on the net asset value of the fund per unit on the day of the dividend payout, and added to the investor's account. Such a model not only removes the hassle of paying an application fee for reinvesting, but also fully demonstrates the effect

of compound interest. Adding accumulated interest to the principal effectively bolsters the actual returns from the fund investment.
Investors must also note that when buying funds they have to verify
dividend reinvestment as their choice for dividend allocation. Otherwise, it may not happen. Regulations binding the fund industry
assume a tacit understanding from the investor that cash dividend
payouts are his or her preferred choice if no verification is provided.

Purchase online to save time and energy

Virtually every bank and fund company out there has set up an
online fund investment entity. Online transactions require very little
manpower and resources, and many offer attractive promotions.
On top of lower fees, online subscription of funds also takes up
substantially less time. That is very attractive to people who are
always in a rush. As the saying goes, time is money.

Stratagem 8

Repair the Walkway Openly but March Secretly to Chéncāng (暗渡陈仓)

Sieve Out Obscure Information in Reports

Origin of the Stratagem

Toward the end of the Qin Dynasty, many powerful figures fought and struggled for domination. Liu Bang's army was the first to enter Guanzhong and invade Xianyang. Subsequently, Xiang Yu charged in with a much larger battalion to force Liu Bang out. At a banquet, Liu Bang survived an assassination attempt to escape with his army to Hanzhong. En route, Liu Bang set fire to the tracks connecting Guanzhong to Hanzhong to cripple Xiang Yu's pursuit, and show his resolve in not returning to Guanzhong. But deep in his heart he was determined to defeat Xiang Yu and take over the throne.

By 206 BC, Liu Bang was a close assistant of the prince, and he sent Han Xin to defend the eastern region. Before he did so, Han Xin sent a battalion to repair the destroyed tracks, making a show of a plan to stage a comeback attack. The news alarmed and alerted the Guanzhong garrisons to keep a close eye on the development. They began to station key units at various checkpoints as a precaution to stymie the Han army's advance. Unbeknownst to them, Han Xin had sent a large troop on a detour through Chéncāng to launch a sneak attack. They defeated Qin General Zhanggan in one swift stroke to take control of Qin territories that were carved up into three parts at the time. It proved to be a critical step in Liu Bang's unification of the Central Plains.

New Spin on Funds

Quarterly reports
Changes in fund holdings
Changes in fund positions
Fund investment portfolios
Special equities

Quarterly reports

After every quarter, all funds will publish their reports on the previous quarter. Investors tend to overlook these reports that may appear difficult to comprehend, but are, in fact, extremely important. Reading and understanding the reports will enable investors to assess and analyze the general trends of the funds and track their performance.

Changes in fund holdings

Quarterly reports will reveal the top 10 holdings of funds in the previous period. An overly large or small fund has an adverse impact on the fluidity of the investment portfolio, the investment style, the degree of investment difficulty, and so on. Similar to an overweight or underweight person, a mega-sized fund worth more than RMB10 (US$1.43) billion, or a mini-sized fund worth around RMB200 (US$28.6) million, should be a red alert. It is also equally important to take note of changes in fund holdings within that quarter, including subscription and redemption of holdings made. They are normally spelled out in the quarterly report. Massive subscription and redemption will put pressure on capital, and prompt fund managers to adjust the positions of funds, which will in turn affect their investment returns.

Changes in fund positions

Changes in fund positions are always indicated in quarterly fund reports. Investors must pay attention to the changes as they shed light on fund managers' forecasts for the next quarter. Fund managers generally tend to have an optimistic short-term market outlook if they are taking long positions on funds, or increasing holdings drastically. Conversely, fund managers who short their positions on funds or cut holdings drastically tend to hold a pessimistic view of the market in the short term. At the end of 2005 when the market was downcast, funds as a whole were lengthening their positions ever so slightly. It was an indication of the fund market's evaluation of the worth of the A-share market, and confidence toward it. From there, investors were also clued in on the market trend and direction.

If the position of the fund you are holding is poles apart from those of similar fund types, alert your fund manager to check whether he or she is "way off the mark," or too "individualistic" in his or her investment style. A fund sometimes goes for longer positions than those of similar fund types to take greater risks in exchange for higher returns. Other funds may adopt positions that work out to be the average of those of similar fund types, and still emerge as frontrunners in their rate of investment return. That, to a certain extent, reflects on the relatively high investment management capability of the fund.

Fund investment portfolios

Quarterly fund reports also list details of the top 10 holdings or heavyweights in funds. They are vital statistics that provide great insights into the investment styles and stock selection processes of various funds. The industries that the heavyweights hail from and their unique features often reflect individual fund managers' preferences for certain holdings. For example, the top 10 holdings in a particular fund comprising mainly blue chips implies a fund investment style that leans toward stability.

Special equity concentration also enables us to determine the dispersion level of fund investment. Special equity concentration is the market value ratio of the top 10 holdings in the fund share investment market value. A relatively high special equity concentration means that the top 10 holdings account for more than half of the fund assets. It also implies that the fund manager has a bias toward concentrated investment, and demonstrates a relatively aggressive investment style.

Special equities

Lastly, pay attention to the continuity of special equities in funds. Compare the list of top 10 holdings published in one quarterly report to the list from the previous quarterly report. A rise in volume in the same stock indicates a greater continuity in special equities, and low fund position adjustments. The reverse is true when the top 10 holdings change every quarter, demonstrating frequent fund position adjustments, and the inclination of the fund manager to go for short-line operation.

Investors should know better than to take the statistics in quarterly fund reports as the gospel truth that tells them everything about their investments. After all, a quarterly report is only good and valid for its statistics recorded right up to the last day of the previous quarter. There is a time lapse and disparity of about 20 days between the public notice announcement and the reorganization of the investment portfolio. During those 20 days, the fund manager could have shifted the holdings on the sly, fooling everyone on his trail. Ultimately, it is crucial for all investors to come to grips with the stock selection process, investment style, and market outlook of each of their fund managers.

Practical tips

Where can you find quarterly reports of funds?

Quarterly reports and information can be sourced through various media channels:

- Newspapers such as *China Securities Journal, Shanghai Securities Journal,* and *Securities Times.*
- Web sites of fund companies, financial information providers, and portal service providers.
- Client relations bank managers.
- Fund investment companies.

Stratagem 9

Observe the Fire from the Opposite Shore
(隔岸观火)

*Adopt a Wait-and-See Attitude During
the Closed Period*

Origin of the Stratagem

In the last few years of the Eastern Han Dynasty, Cao Cao launched an attack against the two brothers Yuan Shang and Yuan Xi, who subsequently escaped to Liaodong to seek refuge with nomadic chieftain Gongsun Kang. All the generals in Cao Cao's camp implored him to raze Liaodong to the ground, and capture the Yuan brothers. Instead of listening to their suggestion, Cao Cao ordered the withdrawal of frontline troops to Xucang to keep an eye on the Liaodong situation quietly.

Meanwhile, Gongsun Kang was concerned that taking the Yuan brothers in could put him in harm's way, even though he heard Cao Cao had returned to Xucang, and harbored no intention of invading Liaodong. Hence, he had soldiers lying in ambush to arrest and behead the Yuan brothers when they arrived to see him in court. Their heads were delivered to Cao Cao, who laughed, and told his men Gongsun Kang had always been fearful and paranoid of territorial aggression from the Yuan brothers.

Cao Cao added that too early an attack from him and his men would have prompted Gongsun Kang to close ranks with the Yuan brothers to fight them. Withdrawing their troops made Gongsun Kang and the Yuan brothers let down their guard, and turn against each other instead. As evident from the outcome, Cao Cao was right.

New Spin on Funds

Ants in your pants
The closed period
Let fund managers do the work
Give new funds the time and space to grow

Ants in your pants

Some newbie fund investors are easily flummoxed by stock market turmoil that causes the net asset value of a fund to take a rollercoaster ride. They are inclined to scurry to the banks to make quick redemptions, only to realize that they cannot do so in the midst of a fund's closed period. It is an extremely unsettling situation for these newbie fund investors to have to witness a perpetual decline in the net asset value of their funds, and be unable to cash in profits. Some newbie investors expect high returns, and constantly compare the new funds they have just bought with old funds, as well as other funds launched during the same period. Inevitably, they whine about the tardy net asset value growth of their funds, and wish fervently that they could switch fund product types, but they are stuck because of the closed period. That gets them all the more agitated.

The closed period

Is the closed period to blame? Whether the closed period is a blessing or a nemesis is open to interpretation. Every new fund comes with a closed period for various reasons. One, it allows the backroom fund operator (registration center) to gear up for fresh daily applications, subscriptions, and redemptions. Two, fund managers can use the closed period to buy shares and bonds with the capital raised as they prepare to make investments.

If a closed period was not imposed, and it was business as usual for subscription and redemption activities, the fund managers' positioning strategy would be in disarray. A closed period allows fund managers to build positions steadily without external interference. It is common for new funds to impose a closed period that prohibits investor subscription or redemption. A reasonably long closed period ensures there is no inflow or outflow of capital to disrupt a fund manager's momentum in building positions.

Investors need not worry about a fund manager extending the closed period indefinitely. As stipulated in "The Measures for the Administration of the Operations of Securities Investment Funds," the closed period can be imposed for no more than three months.

Let fund managers do the work

Fund products generally go for medium- to long-term stable investment returns. Some investors may decide on a redemption based on how a fund performs in the first three months, or some short-term market rumblings. Such a move is not advised as it escalates the costs of transaction, and goes against the grain of long-term investment. In other words, if you are looking at an investment period of less than three months, funds are definitely not the right products for you.

Having picked a new fund to invest in means you accept its investment strategy and philosophy. Stand back and watch from the sidelines. Let your appointed fund manager decide on your behalf when to enter the markets and which shares to pick. Leave him or her to pit his or her skills and wits against other fund managers. Every new fund is required to announce its new asset value weekly, which puts a considerable amount of pressure on the fund manager.

Give new funds the time and space to grow

Be objective about the performance of a new fund, and be patient if you want to see good results. A new fund in its infancy may not have a sizeable ratio in its holdings, thus causing it to experience sluggish net asset value growth, and appear inferior to its older counterparts. On the flip side, a new fund may also have more capital in hand to snap up mainstream and popular products. That kicks net asset value growth into high gear to overtake the frontrunners.

The scenarios and situations change, so it is meaningless to compare new funds that are launched at about the same time. Every new fund builds its positions at a different pace, and every fund manager embraces a different style of managing or operating. A fund that is in the midst of building its positions is also switching the level of its positioning. Hence, it is unwise to compare it excessively with other funds. As we scrutinize the list of top-performing funds or so-called Star Funds, we notice that their performances and ranking within the first six months of their inception were invariably different. Some even came in as laggards. If we had jumped to conclusions about their performance then, we would have missed out on their returns today.

Ultimately, investing in funds requires one to adopt a medium- to long-term perspective. A three-month observation period is far too short for an objective and accurate appraisal. As the Chinese saying goes: "A horse will prove its strength over a distance, just as a person's real character will be revealed over time." So, have patience. Give yourself more time to evaluate your new fund.

Stratagem 10

Hide a Dagger
Behind the Smile
(笑里藏刀)

Beware of Publicity Gimmicks

Origin of the Stratagem

During the Warring States Period, the aggressively expanding Qin State sent Gongsun Yang to invade the Wei State. When Gongsun Yang reached the Wei city of Wucheng, he was delighted to find that his long-time acquaintance Gongzi Xing was the chief commander of the Wei State. Gongsun Yang wasted no time in writing a friendly letter to Gongzi Xing, suggesting that they meet to discuss major matters. Gongsun Yang even followed that up by ordering the Qin troops to withdraw from the frontline.

The letter and the withdrawal of the Qing army swayed Gongzi Xing so much that he immediately wrote a reply to set the date for the discussion. When the day arrived, the atmosphere was cordial. Gongsun Yang reminisced with Gongzi Xing, and even threw a banquet for him. However, just as the latter was about to get into his seat, a siren sounded, and he and his 300-odd delegates were surrounded and captured by soldiers lying in ambush. Gongsun Yang went on to conquer Wucheng by using his prisoners to convince the Wei guards to open the city gate. The Wei State ended up ceding to the Qin State a portion of Xihe, a region west of the Yellow River. Thanks to Gongsun Yang's "daggers behind the smile," the Qin State was able to win for itself a slice of the Yushan territory in Henan province in North China without too much effort.

New Spin on Funds

Look beyond the gloss
Check for legitimacy
Zoom in on the key points
• Types of funds and investment themes matter
• Basis for performance comparison
• Uniqueness of funds
• Back-end and front-end charges
• Ferret out the trappings

Look beyond the gloss

The cunning stratagem of hiding "daggers behind the smile" is not only pervasive on battlegrounds, but also between the pages of a fund's publicity brochure. Let down your guard for a moment and they may pull the wool over your eyes. Piles of such promotional materials of various types of funds can always be found sitting at bank counters. They are neatly arranged and strategically displayed to catch the eyes of all customers. They are refined, the designs exquisite, and the content plentiful. However, you had better look beyond the glossy surface to get to the real substance, and judge for yourself the value of the funds.

Check for legitimacy

Some time back, there was a media report of an incident whereby a bank left "internal communication information" of a fund in the hall for customers to read. It was a grave violation of the law as "internal information" is not regulated by the Supervisory Administration Commission. The content of the "internal information" could well mislead investors. Only officially approved materials ensure the information conveyed is fair, objective, and accurate.

Therefore, when you study publicity materials of funds, first check whether the contents have been officially and legally approved. Beware of a brochure that claims a fund yielded a 150 percent rate of return on a particular day, month, or year without mentioning its performance at other times, or a fund that makes a fuzzy or baseless claim that it is the most successful fund in the industry. They are tell-tale signs that the information given is not only illegitimate but is also the work of an unprofessional firm. Do not let the content deceive you.

Zoom in on the key points

Even legally approved promotional materials can sometimes be difficult to make sense of. There was once a case involving a newly appointed member of the US Securities and Exchange Commission, who had to convert the shares he held as part of his personal assets into funds, as required by the law. But before he could do it, he ran into a snag. He had trouble figuring out the fund contract and the disclosure notice. The situation in China may be comparatively less serious, but it is common to hear people griping about publicity brochures that appear too professional and jargon-ridden. The key to understanding material is not to pore over every word, but to zoom in on the key points.

Types of funds and investment themes matter. The type of fund makes a direct impact on the fund's projected risk and return. In the case of a share-based fund, the law stipulates that it must maintain at least 60 percent holdings in shares, while a composite fund enjoys greater flexibility in terms of the limit for its asset allocation. It is crucial that as a fund investor you are able to tell the difference.

The investment theme of a fund also affects the fund's investment style directly. Most funds that carry the word "growth" in their names invest in new and emerging industries that are experiencing rapid growth. With their tendency to go through spurts of explosive growth, "growth" funds will languish or take a backseat sometimes, especially when blue chips emerge as dominant players. "Growth" funds do not always hog the limelight, or the front rows of the performance ranking.

Basis for performance comparison. Composite funds do not have to abide by any rules with regard to their asset allocation ratios, but we can get a rough idea of that through the basis for performance comparison.

For example, if the basis for performance comparison of a fund is SSE Index Rate of Return × 60 percent + SSE Government Bonds Index Return of Return × 40 percent, it means that the fund has a "neutral asset allocation," with a 60 percent share investment ratio. Any ratio above that percentage is called "high allocation," which implies that the fund is taking a positive view of the current market situation. A ratio below 60 percent is called "low allocation," which indicates that the fund is not so upbeat about the current market situation. Thus, the share investment ratio in the basis for performance comparison is able to give you a fair estimation of the level of return on risk.

Uniqueness of funds. The market is flush with more than 300 funds, with new debutants coming on board every day. Some are unique, such as the Life Cycle Funds. They cater specially to

individuals who have no time to oversee their professional investments, and are preparing for retirement as well as their children's
education.

Other funds in the market may also claim to be unique, and use
words such as "go for the best individual stocks" or "rich pickings
in undervalued individual stocks" to peddle their goods. Logical
as they may sound, dig deeper and you will often find no real
substance to back up the ad claims. Instead, it illustrates the lack
of originality in investment concept and philosophy on the part of
the fund.

Back-end and front-end charges. The rate for fees is another
important aspect to note. Funds that encourage long-term investment usually offer a "back-end application/subscription" payment model. If you intend to make a medium- to long-term
fund investment, go for the back-end payment model. A longer
holding period means lower handling charges. Some funds actually waive the back-end charges after a fixed period of, say, two
years. It is as good as buying a fund free of charge. For investors
making a shorter term fund investment, the rates for fees under
the back-end payment model may actually be higher than those
that come under the front-end payment model. Hence, investors
should take all factors into consideration when buying funds to
determine whether to go with the front-end or the back-end
payment model.

Ferret out the trappings. Investors should also pay attention to
the introductory notes and summaries of the past performances
of funds compiled by the investment research teams. A staggering
amount of information is distilled into publicity brochures and
promotional products for the public. Go through them carefully.
You will find worthy investment information, but may also spot
traps between the lines regarding the investment.

Stratagem 11

Sacrifice a Plum Tree for a Peach Tree
(李代桃僵)

Pay a Price for a Bigger Gain

Origin of the Stratagem

The phrase "sacrifice a plum tree for a peach tree" is derived from the poem "The Crow of a Rooster" in the Yuefu (Music Bureau) Poem Collection. Yuefu holds a compilation of Chinese poems composed in a folk song style.

Literally translated, the poem reads:

Out of a well grows a peach tree
Next to it grows a plum tree
Worms gnaw at the peach roots

The plum takes the place of the peach
Tree for tree in sacrifice
How can such brotherhood be forgotten?

The poem implies that brothers should help out or make sac-rifices for each other in times of difficulty. In military terms, it means paying a small price to secure a big victory when either two opponents are equally matched or you are weaker than your adversary. It is similar to the strategy of "giving up a pawn to save the knight" in a game of chess.

In the late Warring States Period, General Li Mu of the Zhao State insisted on a strategy of defense rather than aggression to keep enemies at the northern gate of Yanmen at bay.

Only a few years after he had strengthened his troops did he decide to mount an attack against the Xiongnu barbarians. Be-fore the actual attack, he dispatched a small legion to protect the shepherds who were taking their flocks out grazing at the border. Just then, a small band of Xiongnu cavalry riders came charging. Li Mu's soldiers immediately feigned defeat by beating a retreat, and leaving some of their men and animals behind. Xiongnu chief-tain Chan Yu thought Li Mu a coward who lacked the courage to venture out of his city to fight his enemies, so he charged straight for Yanmen. While he did that, Li Mu had already deployed his troops to three different locations, waiting for Chan Yu and his men to walk right into their traps. Chan Yu ended up being roundly trounced by Li Mu due to underestimating his ability.

New Spin on Funds

A little damage goes a long way
• Direct or one-off fee payment
• Fund operating fees or period charges
A small price for expert consultation
Take bargains and discounts with a huge pinch of salt

A little damage goes a long way

Fund investors often gripe about exorbitant fees. Some grouch about having to pay more than US$100 in handling fees on top of the other charges for management, custodial, and so on for a US$10,000 fund. Obviously, investors have forgotten that one of the 36 stratagems is about paying a small price for a bigger gain. As the Chinese put it, the essence lies in "capitalizing on advantages and avoiding harm," and "picking the better of two advantages, and choosing the lesser of two evils." It is worthwhile to incur a small loss or price in exchange for a greater victory; an analogy that could be applied to paying the necessary fees for greater returns. Are the fees of funds as expensive as some investors claim them to be? Let's do a bit of calculation here. Open-end funds generally involve two types of fees.

Direct or one-off fee payment.

- **Application and subscription fees**
  An application fee is the handling fee that one pays for buying a fund unit during the launch and offer period of a fund. A subscription fee is the handling fee that one pays for buying a fund during the lockup period. Normally, the application and subscription fees are deducted at the point of fund investment.

  For example, you are prepared to pay US$10,000 for a fund that has just been launched, and the application rate is 1.2 percent. That means for your application of a US$10,000 fund, you will be charged an application fee of US$10,000 − [US$10,000 ÷ (1 + 1.2 percent)] = US$118.58.

  The application fee of a new fund is often lower than the subscription fee as investors are encouraged to apply for the fund. If you invest in a fund during the lockup period, the subscription rate will go up to 1.5 percent. That means paying US$147.78 as an application fee, or an extra US$30 for the same US$10,000 investment in a fund.

- **Redemption fees**

  Never make the mistake of looking upon the net asset value growth of a fund as your profit, as you still have to pay a redemption fee when you decide to bail out of the fund.

  For example, to redeem 1,000 units of the fund for the day's redemption price set at US$1.2 and a redemption rate charge of 0.5 percent, you will have to pay US$1.2 × 1,000 × 0.5 percent = US$6 in redemption fees.

  Different types of funds have different redemption fees. The redemption rate of share-based funds is generally set at 0.5 percent. Bond funds may set theirs as low as zero. Money market funds generally do not charge any redemption fee. However, some guaranteed funds set high benchmarks for premature redemptions. They are penalties of sorts, and are sometimes set higher than 2 percent.

Fund operating fees or period charges. The fund operating fee is necessary to keep the fund in operation. The fee is deducted from the fund assets. That means the investor has to bear the cost of the fee.

- **Fund management fees**

  This is the sole income for the fund management company from your fund investment. The fund management fee is calculated based upon the percentage of net asset value, and the fees vary drastically for funds with unique risk and investment return profiles. The charging rate for money market funds is 0.33 percent, while the rate for bond funds ranges between 0.41 percent and 0.8 percent. Share-based and composite funds usually charge between 0.5 and 1.85 percent. Meanwhile, a unique type of share-based fund, known as an index fund, adopts special strategies that do away with the constant need to switch stocks. Their management fees are generally kept at a rate of 0.75 percent, far lower than those of funds that require active management.

- **Fund custodial fees**

  This is the fee for hiring a custodian to service the fund. An example is the fee that a bank charges to oversee and maintain the trust property of a fund. The custodial fee is based on the net asset value ratio. The rate is 0.25 percent at the time of writing. The annual custodial rate for a money market fund is usually set at 0.1 percent. It is accumulative, and paid to the custodian on a monthly basis by deducting the amount from the fund assets.

- **Other fees**

  Other fees include securities exchange transaction fees, sale service charges, accounting fees, legal fees, fees for shareholders' general assembly, and so on. They are the costs of operating a fund, and are directly deducted from the fund assets.

A small price for expert consultation

If you think about it, the fees of a fund actually do not amount to much. Investing US$1,000 in a share-based fund entitles you to the same privileges enjoyed by many millionaires. It saves you the trouble of having to scrutinize every piece of financial and economic information, or ferret out information left, right, and center.

According to the China Fund Manager Survey Report in April 2004, China fund managers have invested 30,000 hours each in effort. Every one of them has a university education and a postgraduate degree, and more than 90 percent of them are honors degree holders. On average, each of them has worked in the securities industry for 7.7 years, which translates into an average total of 30,000 working hours. Every year, they spend at least an extra 2,000 hours picking potentially good stocks to invest in for you. These fund management professionals also take care of all the nitty-gritty of share transactions for you.

The treatment you are getting is no different from that of a major client. In exchange for such services, the RMB15 (US$2) annual management fee (RMB1,000 × 1.5 percent) that you have to pay is negligible.

Take bargains and discounts with a huge pinch of salt

Last but not least, when you have "bargain" or "special discount" funds dangled in your face like a carrot, recognize them for what they are: mere sales tactics of unimaginative fund managers. Picking a fund that comes with a "special discount" or "bargain" price tag is rarely a wise move.

Funds vary. The subscription fee of most funds is set at 1.5 percent. After the discount that is commonly given, the rate for the handling fee drops to 0.6 percent; that means it is lower by 0.9 percent. What more can you ask for?

At the end of the day, the performance of a fund will be revealed over time. One may go 10 percent higher than another. Over a longer investment period, gains may get duplicated, and create sharp contrasts between funds. In 2006, the best performing share-based fund chalked up a rate of return that was more than three times that of the poorest performer. The moral of the story is, do not let the discounts in handling fees mislead you into choosing fund products that are not suitable for you, or you will commit the crime of being "penny wise, pound foolish."

Practical tips

Table 11.1   Snapshot of the fees for open-end funds (%)

Types of fees	Currency funds	Bond funds	Guaranteed funds	Share-based/ composite funds
Registration	–	0–1.0	0–1.0	0–1.5
Subscription	–	0–1.5	0–1.5	0–2.5
Sales service	0.25	–	–	–
Management	0.33	0.41–0.80	1–1.2	0.5–1.85
Custodial	0.10	0.14–0.2	0.20	0.1–0.35
Redemption	–	0–0.5	0–2.0	0–2.75

Stratagem 12

Seize the Opportunity to Lead a Sheep Away
(顺手牵羊)

Regular Savings Plan

Origin of the Stratagem

In 383 BC, King Fu Jian of the Early Qin State mobilized 900,000 troops to eliminate the Eastern Jin State (317–420 BC). When Fu Jian heard his brother Fu Rong was able to conquer Shouyang in one swift stroke, he decided not to wait for all his troops to return from their different outposts. Instead, he immediately commanded a small army of a few thousand cavalry troops to head straight for Shouyang.

Upon hearing that Fu Jian's million-strong troops had not been assembled in one place, General Xie Shi of Eastern Jin decided to provoke his arrogant opponent into bringing the war to a quick end. He sent a letter calling for a fight to the finish, and goaded Fu Jian to surrender if he did not have the stomach for a showdown. Xie Shi also called for his adversary to back off temporarily to allow him to cross the river for the decisive battle. Fu Jian caved in to the demand, but plotted to crush the Eastern Jin regiment when it was midway across the river. When he ordered his troops to back down, little did Fu Jian expect them to take a beating in spirit and morale. When frustration got the better of the Qin soldiers and pandemonium broke out, Xie Shi ordered his own troops to take the chance to cross the river in double quick time to deal the Qin army a severe and fatal blow.

The spirit that Xie Shi had in taking even the smallest chance won him the battle. It is also in keeping with the Chinese saying "seize the opportunity to lead a sheep away." It means take all chances, even the smallest ones that come our way, as they may help us overcome the biggest obstacles in achieving our goals.

New Spin on Funds

From spare change to fixed savings
Advantages of fixed-income funds
• Bite-sized investment as building blocks • Minimized costs and risks • Auto payment saves time and effort • Affordable and low starting point
Complementary fixed-investment tools

From spare change to fixed savings

Every one of us spends a fair amount of pocket money every month. A trip to a restaurant, a few packets of cigarettes, and other miscellaneous expenses easily add up to a few hundred dollars. Perhaps you should think about saving some of this money "along the way" for an investment, such as a fixed-income fund, that may just bring you a windfall.

Capital time value and the duplication effect illuminate the accumulated effect of an investment. A small investment every month adds up to a lot over time, and may eventually become a hefty sum. According to statistics, share-based funds (with composite funds in the mix) in China reported a sterling 22.48 percent annual average rate of return from 1998 to 2006, despite the bearishness of the markets from 2001 to 2005.

Fixed-income funds do not enter the stock markets. That is obviously fine by investors who feel awkward about joining the fray. For them, fixed-income funds make the simplest, most attractive, and most effective medium- to long-term fund investments.

Advantages of fixed-income funds

Bite-sized investment as building blocks. Fixed-income funds are similar to banking fixed deposits by installments as they serve both as a form of savings and investment. Every month, invest a fixed amount of capital in a particular fund over an extended period. The money will grow and become a sizeable fortune.

Minimized costs and risks. No matter how tumultuous the market situation is, a fixed amount of money is regularly invested in the fund. It is a way to capitalize on bargains and avoid risks. Regular investment and fixed amount are two prerequisites for small purchases when the net asset value of the fund is high, and big purchases when the net asset value is low. A wave band operation is difficult to manage successfully, but an "enforced" tactic by way of regular fixed investment promotes consistency. Over an extended period, the method diminishes costs and risks.

Auto payment saves time and effort. You can apply with the sale agent or company to arrange for regular payments to be deducted from your stated capital account, by setting the date and time, the sum, and the method of payment. It is convenient, and saves time as well as energy.

Affordable and low starting point. The starting minimum sum is usually set at RMB200 (US$29) to RMB500 (US$71), lower than a one-off investment. Hence, you can easily use your monthly pocket money to invest in fixed-income funds. What about the larger amount of capital that is lying idle? Should you use it to make a one-off investment, or regular fixed investment? A one-off investment will do better than regular fixed investment if it is a bull market your fund is investing in. Conversely, regular fixed investment is the way to go to spread out and lower the impact of your investment risk in a market that is undergoing consolidation.

Complementary fixed-investment tools. Of course you can combine one-off investment and regular fixed investment to realize your medium- to long-term financial goals. The two are complementary investment tools. One-off investment involves the management of current capital savings, while regular fixed investment is tied to the management of future monthly cash flow. You can start off by using your idle capital to make a one-off investment in a fund, before investing part of your income in a regular fixed investment on a monthly basis.

The fund company plays a key role in determining the funds to pick for your regular fixed investment. Therefore, pick a fund company with a proven record in delivering stable and sustainable results. Next, identify the various types of funds that are suitable for your investment. Generally, share-based funds that fluctuate more in their results are best suited for regular fixed investment, as they demonstrate the greatest ability in curtailing risks.

Practical tips

The keys to regular fixed investment

1. The biggest draw about regular fixed investment is that it evens out investment costs. Share-based funds or composite funds make the best types of regular fixed-investment funds. Bond funds and money market funds

provide fixed returns, so their risk factor impact is less obvious.

2. To boost the uptake of regular fixed investment, some fund management companies have introduced special discounts on fees and special investment arrangements for regular fixed-investment clients. Investors are usually able to enjoy lower rates for application fees, and they can apply to buy more fund holdings at the eleventh hour, just before the deadline for application closes.

3. Regular fixed investment requires a relatively long investment period to minimize the impact of short-term volatility on investment returns. If an investor, for some reason, is unable to put up with a market unraveling in the short run, and wishes to redeem or pull out of a regular fixed-investment fund, he or she may incur losses, or not achieve the goal of spreading out the costs of a regular fixed investment over a long period.

Stratagem 13

Beat the Grass to Startle the Snake (打草惊蛇)

See Through the Fund Management Company

Origin of the Stratagem

The stratagem "beat the grass to startle the snake" has a double meaning. One implies the need to act with caution so as not to alert a lurking enemy to one's intentions, or cause it to make the first move. The second meaning underlines the use of a stick to rattle and trap a snake.

In 627 BC, Qin Mugong planned to conquer the Zheng State and subdue its capital city with the help of a spy he had planted there. The Qin State's top advisor Jian Shu was against the war, and warned of a potentially unsuccessful mission. He voiced his fear that the Qin army might end up getting ambushed and wiped out by the Jin State troops in Yushan. As Jian Shu predicted, the Zheng State kicked the Qin spy out of its kingdom, and was all geared up for combat after finding out about Qin's planned attack. The foiled plan forced the Qin army to head back home, but the march was long and arduous. Meanwhile, the heavily armed Jin troops were lying in ambush in the hills and valleys in Yushan. They gave the Qin army a good drubbing, and captured Qin General Meng Mingshi alive.

The Qin army had alerted the enemy, and caused its own downfall by failing to check on the enemy's situation, and acting rashly. It had, in effect, rattled the "snake" into making an aggressive strike. In the military, "rattling the snake" is also a tactic used to lure an enemy out of its hiding place, so as to make it easier to capture.

New Spin on Funds

> **Picking a reliable fund company**
> * Telling signs around us
> * Ask the dumb questions
> * Quiz the customer hotline service representative

Picking a reliable fund company

You always begin the search for your desired fund products with the fund company you choose to work with. To a certain degree, picking a fund company is more important than choosing a fund product since the fund company will be charged with managing the product. To find the fund company that fits the bill, you have to check its past performance records, internal audit capability, and governance mechanism. A fund company that stands on solid and robust ground in these three areas is usually one that puts investors' interests first.

Telling signs around us. A fund company's internal audit capability and governance mechanism are often kept out of the public eye, and you may find it a challenge to pry into them. In such a case, the best approach is to sound out finance management professionals in the fund company for some clues. As the Chinese saying goes: "The fall of a leaf spells the dawn of autumn while a stream leads one to the sea." That means there are signs that you can read from what is happening around you.

For a start, take the Guiding Opinions on the Internal Control of Securities Investment Fund Sale Institutions as a reference point. It ordains that the sale and promotion of funds should adhere to the principles of honesty and honor, and should not set out to cheat or mislead investors. They should also take into account an investor's risk tolerance level, and his or her compatibility with the risk/return of a fund product.

Ask the dumb questions. You may want to dress up as a totally ignorant newbie investor, and ask financial management professionals some "stupid" questions, such as whether they sell cheap funds. They may just give you an affirmative answer, tell you the net asset value of their funds is a bargain at only US$1 each, and comparatively cheaper than their competitors' which are US$3 each, with no room to rise further. Do not ever fall for the words or guise of such fund managers (as illustrated in Stratagem 1). Watch out for salespeople with the tendency to mislead investors. They also point to signs of poor supervision and management within their companies.

Quiz the customer hotline service representative. The customer hotline of a fund company can also clue you in on its management standards. The telephone customer service is a reflection of not only the quality and standard of the customer service representative, but also the company's team philosophy, work efficiency, and level of inter-departmental coordination. The customer service representative is tasked mainly with disseminating information pertaining to the results delivered by the other departments in the company. Inaccurate and untimely customer service information is a sign of operational hiccups in the fund company.

Pretend to be a fussy customer, and ask a variety of questions related to application, subscription, redemption, investment, innovative products, fund swaps, dividends, shareholder changes, background of fund managers, and so forth. If the customer service representative cannot provide clear answers, or information beyond what you already know, the service quality and management standard of the company are questionable.

Ultimately, when we pick funds to invest in, the management of a fund company, the risk controls, internal audit, and many more fundamental factors are all important elements to take into consideration. Of course, it is never easy for an investor to probe into the fundamentals of a fund company, so the best approach is to "create some noise" in order to get the company to reveal its true colors.

Stratagem 14

Borrow a Corpse to Raise the Spirit (借尸还魂)

Innovation Adds New Value

Origin of the Stratagem

The Chinese proverb "borrow a corpse to raise the spirit" means using some method to revive the dead. In the military, it refers to a strategy of employing insignificant powers to attain one's goals.

During the reign of the second Qin emperor from 211 BC to 207 BC, Chen Sheng and Wu Guang were drafted to guard the Yuyang border. Heavy downpours often flooded the roads at Daze Village, making it difficult for the two border guards to reach Yuyang in time. However, the Qin government decreed they must show up on time or face execution. This angered Chen Sheng and

Wu Guang, who would rather fight for survival than take such a decree lying down. This gave them cause for an uprising.

However, Chen Sheng thought his lowly status would not allow him to rally effectively for an uprising. At the time, there were two prominent men who commanded the respect of the masses. One of them was Fu Su, the amicable and benevolent oldest son of Emperor Qin Shihuang (259 BC–210 BC) who had been murdered by the scheming and ruthless second Qin emperor. The masses were kept in the dark about his death. The other person was Chu General Xiang Yan, who won many accolades and enjoyed a tremendous reputation. However, his whereabouts were a mystery ever since the Qin State annexed six other states, namely Han in 233 BC, Zhao in 228 BC, Yan in 227 BC, Wei in 225 BC, Chu in 223 BC, and Qi in 221 BC.

Chen Sheng decided to use Fu Su and Xiang Yan to rally mass support. He conferred upon himself the title of General, and Wu Guang the title of Commander. His call for support drew enormous responses far and wide. Eventually, Chen Sheng's followers honored him with the imperial title of King Zhang Chu.

New Spin on Funds

Death of a dated fund
A breath of new life
• Features of innovative close-end funds
Makeover feasibility

Death of a dated fund

"Borrow a corpse to raise a spirit" sounds spooky, but you have nothing to be afraid of. It is merely an analogy to the effect of "turning something mediocre into a miracle." An innovative close-end fund is a case in point.

Since their launch in 2001, open-end funds have gained widespread market acceptance, and are hugely popular with investors. It was a stark contrast for close-end funds. For a long time, no new close-end funds were launched. Everyone seemed to have forgotten about them. There were reasons for this. For one, close-end funds lacked liquidity. Any investor who wants to bail out or cash in profits has to sell his or her funds on the stock exchanges. Furthermore, the fund's net asset value and the trading supply and demand levels put a cap on the transaction price. The price is often much higher in relation to the net asset value of a fund, and therefore unacceptable to the investor. (See Stratagem 26 for a detailed look at close-end funds.)

A breath of new life

By 2007, close-end funds had shed their stuffy image as innovative close-end funds debuted, one after another. The earlier cold shoulder treatment was replaced by a warm market reception.

These funds came with two innovative features.

Features of innovative close-end funds. First of all, a close-end fund is able to change its operating format if its discount rate surpasses a certain level after a fixed period following its trading debut. For example, if its discount rate exceeds 20 percent after 50 consecutive trading days, it can be converted into a listed open-end fund or LOF to accept redemption applications from investors. This ensures investors can make redemptions based on the net asset value of the fund, without having to enter the secondary market for transactions that may undermine their positions. This is known as a "lifeboat clause."

Secondly, an innovative close-end fund is structurally divided into many levels. Normally, every fund holding enjoys equity in privileges and obligations. However, some innovative close-end funds have created a stratified framework, separating fund holdings into a priority class tranche and an ordinary class tranche. Capital is raised, and prices are set separately for the two stratified holdings, but the assets come together to work as one. It is a single entity in the eyes of the law.

The basic difference between the two strata is that the priority class tranche enjoys priority allocation rights. That means profits are first distributed to the priority class tranche before the remaining income is distributed to the ordinary class tranche. The priority class tranche is endowed with stability and sustainability, and is similar to lower class bonds in risk and returns. The ordinary class tranche takes the "leftovers" in profit distribution, but at times yields a higher ratio of return over the holdings. Hence, a stratified fund is able to offer asset growth opportunities simultaneously to both steady and aggressive investors.

Let's say a US$1,000 investment in a priority class tranche has made a profit of US$100 after a year; a profit ratio of 5 percent means that US$5 will be distributed to you. The rest of the US$95 will be calculated based on the ratio of one to nine, which means you will get US$9.5 out of it, while the remaining US$85.50 will be distributed to ordinary class tranche holders. Therefore, a priority class tranche may have made US$100, but at the end of the day, its investor is awarded only US$14.50. The remaining US$85.50 goes to the ordinary class tranche holders who have to shoulder more investment risks. It is an arrangement that fits the bill for both parties.

An ordinary class tranche certainly has the potential to yield a higher ratio of return over the holdings, but a bull market can sometimes do a lot of damage. An ordinary class tranche investor is therefore required to have a stronger stomach for risk, and greater psychological resilience.

Makeover feasibility

Innovative close-end funds have retained some of the unique qualities of traditional close-end funds in terms of being publicly held and traded on the stock exchanges, being stable in size, allowing 100 percent ownership in shares, and so on. They have also incorporated many positive features from open-end funds, such as allowing redemption to be made in net asset value as long as certain conditions have been fulfilled. The seemingly complicated strata system is, in fact, a flexible one that enables a fund to take on the functions of many. Innovative close-end funds have breathed new life into the "spirit" of asset management and traditional close-end funds that almost faded into obscurity at one point.

No matter what form innovation takes, an investment product depends very much on its performance result in relation to the risk level for survival, which in turn has to be backed by an effective investment strategy, excellent management standards, and a feasible investment philosophy. There is no such thing as a good or bad product in the investment market, only what is feasible or not feasible.

Stratagem 15

Lure the Tiger Down the Mountain (调虎离山)

Move "Risks" Out of the Way

Origin of the Stratagem

In the last few years of the Eastern Han Period, Sun Ce wanted to topple warlord general Liu Xun who had Hujiang under his occupation. However, Sun Ce knew a head-on clash would not produce victory, so he and his generals devised a strategy to lure Liu Xun away from his stronghold, a tactic borrowed from the Chinese concept of "luring a tiger down the mountain."

Sun Ce started off by sending Liu Xun an expensive gift, and appearing weak before seeking his help to fight Shangliao's aggression. Completely taken in, Liu Xun personally led tens of thousands of troops to Shangliao, leaving Hujiang open and vulnerable to Sun

79

Ce's assault. Faced with little resistance, Sun Ce seized control of Hujiang with ease.

The point here is, Sun Ce not only managed to lure the enemy away from its stronghold, but also to a territory favorable to his military to secure the ultimate victory.

New Spin on Funds

Harness your advantages
- Investments suitable for the young
- Investments suitable for the middle-aged
- Investments suitable for the aged

Harness your advantages

Sun Ce decided to attack the city because he was highly jealous of Liu Xun for having a well-fortressed city with a moat guarded by a strong army of soldiers. As Sun Ce staked his claim on the city, Liu Xun could only run for his life, and watch helplessly as his grain supplies, his riches, and his people fell into enemy hands. Liu Xun regretted not defending the resources that were so precious to him.

Making an investment is just like fighting a war. You need to know where your advantages and disadvantages are. Take your eyes off them momentarily, and you may find yourself in the same position as Liu Xun. If you are easily distracted by a carrot dangled in front of you, you may lose your advantage without even knowing it. Like the clever strategist Sun Ce, a smart investor will know how to harness his or her advantages, capitalize on the uniqueness of a product, and make feasible adjustments to realize investment goals.

A special feature of funds is that they come in all shapes and sizes, tagged with a wide array of investment themes. When you are just starting out in your investment, you face a bombardment of choices. It is an academic exercise simply to decide on the types of funds to invest in, the amount to invest, and the time of entry into the market. From a professional point of view, we usually suggest that an investor follow the life cycle of each fund to decide his or her portfolio. Making adjustments and allocations to different types of funds at different times will enable an investor to balance his or her profit and risk.

Investments suitable for the young. Young people have the great advantage of having time on their side. From the first day of work to the day of retirement, it is an investment period that could span as long as 40 years; enough for one to experience several complete economic cycles, and enjoy many more opportunities to reap the rewards of economic growth. Therefore, young people have the greatest ability to fend off risk. As some people would put it, they "can afford to lose." That is why we are inclined to advise young people to invest more of their capital in share-based funds, in the range of 70 percent to 80 percent of their total fund investment. A bull market can often bring them higher-than-average returns, but a bear market will require them to pay a higher price than more conservative investors. Nevertheless, a long investment period ensures that returns from the market will average out to a fair amount for these young investors. As the China stock markets have a relatively short history, let's draw examples from overseas markets. For 20 years right up till December 31, 2005, the average annualized rate of return for the US Standard & Poor's 500 Index stood at 12 percent. If we take it as a 12 percent annual growth and duplicate it, an initial US$1,429 investment will expand to US$14,286 after 20 years. You must give it time and have the patience to make this happen. At the same time, you have to stay resilient, and not be knocked out of play by any market mayhem in the process.

Investments suitable for the middle-aged. With the passage of time, turning middle-aged often makes a person steadier and

looking for more stability. Imminent retirement and family bur-
dens also deter a middle-aged person from taking too many risks.
However, relative wealth built up over the years is the edge that is
created. It minimizes risks. Ensuring stable capital growth should
be the ultimate investment goal of any middle-aged person. At this
stage, a middle-aged person should reduce investments in share-
based funds and increase holdings in bond funds.

Abiding strictly by a stipulated ratio for share-based fund and
bond fund investment can help you to realize your goals more easily.
Assume you have made plans to allot a 5:5 ratio in investment to
share-based funds and bond funds. But then, a bull run in the
market rendered share-based fund prices higher a year later, well
ahead of bond funds. If the ratio works out to 6:4, you should
redeem your share-based fund, and buy into bond funds to regain
the 5:5 ratio. If a bear market causes shares to plummet and flips
the ratio around to 4:6, redeem bond funds and buy into share-
based funds to reinstate the 5:5 ratio. It is a process of selling
high and buying low that minimizes losses, and promotes steady
asset growth.

Investments suitable for the aged. In your golden years, you
would have accomplished most of your goals in life, from owning
a property to seeing that your children receive a proper education,
and so on. It would be your biggest wish to keep your capital safe
and be able to enjoy life, and bond funds are the best instrument
to help you realize that. It is almost impossible to lose money in a
bond investment. Bond funds make dispersed investments in central bank coupons, government bonds, and other more reputable
bonds that reinforce the efforts to keep risk at bay. Investing in convertible bonds, corporate bonds, and other similar types of bonds
simultaneously may also generate a greater rate of return. If you
are more concerned about security than profit, bond funds are the
best investments for you. Give share-based funds a wide berth as
they involve higher risk.

Stratagem 16

To Catch Something, First Let It Go (欲擒故纵)

Be Fully Prepared Before Casting Your Die

Origin of the Stratagem

Shu-Han Chancellor Zhuge Liang's (181 BC–234 BC) capture and release of Meng Huo seven times in succession is a classic example of the Chinese military stratagem of "to catch something, first let it go."

After the founding of the Shu-Han State, the kingdom which was also known as the Shu State mapped out an ambitious plan to make an incursion into the north. Coincidentally, the chieftain of the Southwest Plains, Meng Huo, commandeered 100,000 troops to invade the Shu State. Zhuge Liang responded by mobilizing key troops to take up positions, and lay in ambush in the valleys near Lushui, which is the present-day Jinsha River. Goaded into facing the challenge, Meng Huo and his men walked right into the enemy's trap.

However, Zhuge Liang was mindful of the tremendous power and influence that Meng Huo had over the Southwest Plains. Zhuge believed getting Meng Huo to surrender voluntarily was the best way to ensure the stability of the south, otherwise the Shu State would continue to face bombardment from the various tribes in the Southwest Plains. From then on, Zhuge Liang decided to play a mind game with Meng Huo by freeing him and taking him prisoner following each battle. In the final crossfire, Zhuge Liang set fire to Meng Huo's rattan-armored warriors, and captured him again. On the seventh time that he was arrested and released, Meng Huo thanked Zhuge Liang for sparing his life, and swore he would not attack the Shu State anymore.

With peace and stability secured in the southwestern region of the Shu State, Zhuge Liang was then able to proceed with his plan to make an incursion into the north.

New Spin on Funds

The danger of luck
Know thyself, know thine enemy
Hard work and patience pay off

The danger of luck

It is rare for the general of an enemy's troops to be released once he has been captured. For Zhuge Liang to do that seven times in a row was even more unusual. His purpose was to capture the "hearts" of the people, rather than to show off his exceptional skills in taking enemies prisoner. Had he and the Shu army beheaded Meng Huo right away upon winning the battle, there would have been no peace in the southwestern region.

We can draw parallels from such a situation with the purchase of a fund. A good friend may call to alert you to a limited fund promotion at a bank, and urge you to queue up for it before it is too late. In another case, a friend may urge you to snap up a fund on rumors that it is open for more subscriptions because the market has tumbled in two successive sessions. For all we know, this friend may be a strategist who is as shrewd as Zhuge Liang, or as masterful as Zhang Fei. The investor may succeed in securing some funds, and making a tidy sum through market speculation. However, that is nothing to be smug about. The investor should give some serious thought as to whether, from a long-term perspective, he or she has made the right choice, and bought the right product for himself or herself.

Just like in war, soldiers have to analyze where they stand against their enemies, and find out their capabilities before combat. It will take sheer luck to win a battle if you do it in a haphazard manner, without getting a handle on the situation. Likewise, a hasty investment decision based on the allure of an advertisement or a friend's hearsay can be dicey. You may come to regret it.

Know thyself, know thine enemy

An advertisement or a friend's advice is like a war bulletin's alert to an imminent enemy attack. It spells the need for more research and preparation work. Sun Tzu's saying "know thyself, know thine enemy" is as equally applicable to a fund investor as to a war strategist.

Find out more about the background of the fund companies you are planning to engage. Are they joint ventures or domestic-funded enterprises? What types of fund products have they launched? How have their existing ranges of fund products performed over the years? What are their historical records like? Who are the fund managers responsible for the products you are looking to buy? What are their backgrounds and track records? How are the products classified? Do they match your current financial investment and management needs? These are just a few of the questions you should raise.

You can find some of the answers, such as the details of some fund products, in several mainstream financial and securities newspapers. Investors who can get online should surf the Web sites of the fund companies to gather the relevant information, or check out some mainstream fund-investment-related Web sites, or investigate the opinions of fund investors on forum-based Web sites. The easiest way is to call the customer service of fund companies (note: not the phone numbers of banks that are only acting as sales agents). From a telephone operator, you will not only obtain the information you need, but you will also be able to judge from his or her tone the company's level of professionalism, work efficiency, management situation, and so on.

An investor as smart as Zhuge Liang will do more than that. He or she will observe and gather information about the fund company that he or she covets. If the company is organizing a briefing on its investment and financial management status, this provides a great opportunity for investors to interact with the company fund specialists and managers, or simply to be on the ground to observe the company's activities.

Hard work and patience pay off

Attending such an event can be time and energy consuming, taking hours, or days, or longer. You may have to do it at the expense of some other potential investments or bargains. It is fine to "miss the boat" with investment opportunities that promise only meager gains. Also, look upon this as a chance to sit back until there is a chance for you to make greater advances or strides in your investments.

Investing in funds is all about investing in people. They are the folks you have hired to help you pick stocks. Hence, it is of the utmost importance that you do background checks on the people and fund companies you are hiring or engaging, to ensure you can truly trust them with your money. From a long-term point of view, the integrity of the fund and the quality of the fund managers matter much more than the fund's effectiveness in delivering results.

Stratagem 17

Toss a Brick
to Draw a Gem
(抛砖引玉)

The Art of Turning Mediocrity into Gold

Origin of the Stratagem

The Chinese saying "toss a brick to draw a gem" is taken from Chuandeng Lu or the Transmission of the Lamp, which chronicles the development of Chinese lexicons and semantics. Tang poet Chang Jian was said to have once invited a fellow poet Zhao Gu to write a poem together. Chang Jian kicked off by penning two phrases on a temple wall. Zhao Gu followed up with two lines that were even more brilliant than Chang Jian's. Subsequently, scholars allude to Chang Jian's actions as a manner of "casting a brick to draw a gem." Militarily speaking, it refers to the use of a disguise or decoy to confuse and fool an enemy into submission.

91

In 700 BC, the Chu State used this strategy to overrun the city of Jiao. Some soldiers disguised as woodcutters went into the hills, tempting enemy soldiers into robbing them of the logs they had gathered. The bait worked, drawing more enemy soldiers out of the city of Jiao into the woods, and into the traps set up by the Chu army. Numerous enemy soldiers were killed in the bloodbath, and the king of Chu took the opportunity to invade the city of Jiao. Knowing he was trapped, the marquis of Jiao surrendered without any resistance.

New Spin on Funds

A simple test method
Tell-tale signs in service
Creating a respectable portfolio

A simple test method

Some investors pinch and save to invest their money in funds, even though they may not have any inkling what funds are all about. It is not unheard of to have investors asking bank executives for the interest rate of a certain fund that they have just subscribed to.

When making an investment, never assume that every fund company is the same, or expect a single recommendation to guarantee you the best deal. Ideally, you should have all the facts at your fingertips even before you invest. Some people have made noise about the complexity of funds. Indeed, the market comes with more than 50 fund companies, 300-odd funds, and a copious flow of new funds. It can be an intimidating task trying to make head or tail of them all, and figure out your most suitable choice. But spending time to find out more about these funds will enable you to put a long-term sound financial management plan in place.

The simplest and most direct way is to invest a small amount of money in a few funds that you like. It is a test method that the Chinese call "tossing a brick to draw a gem." You begin by making a paltry investment; let's say US$1,000, which is the minimal sum applicable to most funds. Nevertheless, it entitles you to the same privileges enjoyed by other investors. Rather than relying on hearsay, tap these privileges for a first-hand understanding of the management capability, the quality of service, and professional standard of a fund company.

We tend to pay scant attention to matters that do not concern us. However, once you have a stake in a fund, no matter how big or small, you will start to pay close attention to the rise and fall of the net asset value, changes in the holdings in heavyweights, news about the company, and so on. This should strike a chord with investors who have "been there, done that." The experience will deepen your interest and knowledge unconsciously in the various types of fund companies. You will learn on your own to discover funds that fit in with your investment targets and style the most, and broaden your investment.

Tell-tale signs in service

Performance is not the only benchmark of an excellent fund company. Customer service is another telling area.

First, professionalism should be demonstrated in the service. It becomes clear in the way a customer service representative is able to provide timely and professional answers to the questions you have raised about the performance of funds, the markets, and the procedures involved in all aspects of dealings. The second point pertains to the timeliness of service, which is all about a fund company's agility in reacting swiftly to an abrupt turn of market events, and passing on the information to customers. Third on the list is value-added service, such as whether customers are able to receive relevant investment information on a regular basis. The next point concerns how safe the provided service is. Is the transaction system of the company safe and stable? Will there be more opportunities for a new customer to interact face-to-face with fund managers and the management down the road? Being able to get to all this information will reveal to you the management efficiency and service standard of a company.

Creating a respectable portfolio

As you pick up more funds, you are in fact building a portfolio for yourself. After a trial period, you may find these funds are truly unique, and match your profit and risk criteria. Congratulations are in order. You have stumbled onto a fairly respectable investment portfolio that contains a diversity of fund products and companies. It will enable you to spread out the risk, and enjoy the special services and privileges offered by various fund companies. However, bail out early if you find any of the products dissatisfying. A more prudent way is to focus your energy on becoming a VIP client of fund companies that you truly trust.

Stratagem 18

Nab the Bandits to Capture the Ringleader (擒賊擒王)

Cover Key Funds to Cover All Grounds

Origin of the Stratagem

The Chinese saying "hit 'em where it hurts most" also exists in English. In the military context, it is "nab the bandits to capture the leader." The phrase is adapted from Tang poet Du Fu's poem "Moving out of the Frontier Pass."

The poem reads:

The bow you draw should be strong
The arrow you use should be long
Shoot at his horse before the horseman
Capture the brigand chief before his men

The poem is simple and easy to understand. Hitting out at your adversary's most vulnerable spot is the most effective way to overcome your obstacle.

During the Anshi Rebellion in 755 AD in the Tang Dynasty, General An Lushan's able rebel commander Yin Ziqi led an elite squad to invade Suiyang. Garrison commander-in-chief Zhang Xun was a man of great cunning. Upon seeing the formidable contingent heading his way, he decided to bide his time till night-fall when Yin Ziqi's forces were worn out before staging a surprise counter-attack. Zhang Xun intended to strike at the heart of the problem by confronting Yin Ziqi directly. However, they had never met, and it would be difficult for Zhang Xun to identify Yin Ziqi in frenzied warfare.

Suddenly, Zhang Xun thought of the idea of getting his soldiers to shave arrows out of straw sticks to use against the enemy soldiers. When Yin Ziqi's soldiers discovered they were merely straw-stick arrows, they were convinced Zhang Xun's troops had run out of real arrows. So they ran to deliver the good news to Yin Ziqi. Immediately, Zhang Xun spotted Yin Ziqi, and ordered his troops to aim their arrows at him. Shot in the left eye, Yin Ziqi and his soldiers fled the scene with their tails between their legs.

New Spin on Funds

Find your dream fund
• Higher returns
• Lower risk
• Best of both worlds

Find your dream fund

Zhang Xun had made "nabbing the bandits to capture the ringleader" his core strategy right from the very beginning. Coming up with an ingenious method to identify and zoom in on his target promptly enabled Zhang Xun to outmaneuver the rebel commander Yin Ziqi in a single effective move. If not for this, Zhang Xun's comparatively small army could not have snuck up on the enemy. They would have been beaten by the enemy.

You may want to learn from Zhang Xun, and sift out the fund that best fits your needs and helps you accomplish your investment goals. You may want to take a step back, and think of ways to get the fund to reveal itself to you amid all the choices that are available.

Higher returns. Zoom in on the rate of return. Some people covet and invest in the fund that rings in the highest quarterly or monthly rate of return. However, they will soon realize that the top rankings change nearly every month. Unlike shares, an open-end fund seldom rises more than 10 percent in a day even though the trading costs may reach a high of 2 percent. So be warned, adopting a myopic mode of investing in funds that is similar to share speculation will make you lose out big.

There is also no guarantee that a fund that tops the ranking in one year will have a place in the top three positions the following year. Do not commit the mistake of looking purely at the rate of return, and end up making all the wrong assumptions. The risk exposure and returns are often among the highest for share-based funds, followed by composite funds, and then bond funds. It is therefore unfair to make such direct comparisons between all the different fund types.

You will also get only a miniscule lead by looking at the short-term performance rankings. Generally speaking, a market cycle takes three years or more to complete, and the period often comes with a mix of bull and bear runs, as well as upward and downward gyrations. Thus, you have to track at least three years of performance in order to pinpoint the top performer.

Lower risk. Some investors buy funds to offset the huge risk borne by a single stock in a volatile market. This is a judicious move.

As mentioned before, the net asset value of a fund accelerates and decelerates slower than a share. Given the limit set for shareholdings, the net asset value of even the most aggressive funds fluctuates at an average range of 90 percent to 95 percent if you compare it with that of the stock market.

So how do we look at the risk of funds? We normally use the fluctuation rate of a fund as a barometer. A relatively small net value fluctuation rate means the fund faces low risk, and theoretically is less susceptible to a downtrend. The rate of fluctuation is difficult to calculate, and you do not have to do it yourself. MorningStar, Galaxy Securities, and professional fund ratings organizations publish the fluctuation rates of various funds on a regular basis. From there, you can judge for yourself their downtrend resistance. Whenever a market enters an adjustment period, look closely at funds that experience the least downward fluctuations, and compare them with other funds of the same categories and types.

Over a period of observation, you will be able to narrow down your search for "Yin Ziqi," or the top performer. Bear in mind that effective comparisons can only occur if you are looking at the same types of funds.

The best of both worlds. How do you achieve high returns with low risk? Choose a good fund that not only regulates risk and produces outstanding results, but also keeps fluctuations within a tolerable scope. The Sharpe Ratio is a useful barometer of excess return per unit of total risk return, which is the rate of return that a fund provides on the same level of risk. A high Sharpe Ratio signifies a substantial rate of return. Professional organizations publish this information regularly. Through the Sharpe Ratio, you can find a fund that performs above average consistently, if not spectacularly. More importantly, you won't make the mistake of picking one that gives you heart-thumping moments as it nosedives.

Practical tips

Rating criteria of fund rating organizations

Going by their star rankings, MorningStar, Lipper, and China Galaxy Securities all use the accounting rate of return evaluation index, the risk evaluation index, and risk-adjusted return evaluation index in different measures and compositions.

1. MorningStar
- Rating basis: MorningStar calculates the risk-adjusted return by taking into account both the rate of return and investment risks. It will then rank funds of the same category and type according to the size of their risk-adjusted return, from high to low. The number of stars awarded determines the ratings; five being the best.
- Procedures in ratings:
    a. Identify the categories.
    b. Evaluate the rate of return.
    c. Tally up the risk-adjusted return.
    d. Award stars to funds according to their ratings. Five stars represent the top performer, and the number goes down from there.

2. Lipper
- Rating basis: Lipper classifies funds into five lots. The top 20 percent make up the first lot, marked by a tick. Those ranging from 21 percent to 40 percent comprise the second lot, and are represented by a "2." The list goes down from there. That means the lot holding funds in the range of 81 percent to 100 percent gets a "5" marking.

- Evaluation criteria: They include the total rate of return, steady returns, the break-even point, and fee charges. Lipper's rate of return evaluation index keys in on the total rate of return and steady returns, while its risk evaluation index studies the break-even point and steady returns. Its risk/return index indicates a fund's risk/returns at different points over a specific period, unlike most other risk indices that only look at a single time frame.

3. *China Galaxy Securities Research Center*
- Rating basis: It is largely similar to how MorningStar and Lipper employ the rate of return evaluation index, the risk evaluation index, and the risks returns index in a package.

When a fund's rate of return evaluation index is being conducted, China Galaxy also takes into consideration the fund's net asset value (NAV), quarterly NAV, and monthly NAV. Subsequently, each NAV is converted into a benchmark. The higher the benchmark, the higher the rate of return enjoyed by the fund.

As for the risk evaluation index, the difference in benchmark derived from the monthly NAV is transformed into a score for evaluation. Meanwhile, the risk/return index takes into account both the evaluations on the fund's rate of return and risk. The evaluation score for the rate of return minus the evaluation score for risk produces the score for risk/return. A higher benchmark for risk/return shows a fund delivering better overall performance.

Stratagem 19

Rake the Firewood from Under the Pot (釜底抽薪)

Reasons for Selling Funds

Origin of the Stratagem

The Chinese idiom "rake the firewood from under the pot" was coined by Wei Shou of Northern Qi. He wrote a passage entitled "Stop the boiling by removing the fire and remove the weeds by taking out the roots."

It is similar to another ancient saying:

Add water to stop the boiling
Alas, the boiling will not stop
Get to the root of the issue
Remove the fire and the boiling shall stop

The idea is simple and easy to grasp. When the water is boiling, adding more water will not lower the water temperature much. The fire needs to be removed for the water temperature to drop significantly. In a military context, it means a strategy of avoiding a head-on clash with a strong adversary, and steering clear of an adversary's challenge to put a damper on its combatant mood before seizing an opportunity to triumph over the enemy.

In the late Eastern Han Period, Cao Cao had only slightly more than 20,000 soldiers to defend Guandu against Yuan Shao's 100,000-strong forces. Clearly outnumbered, Cao Cao knew he could not face a direct confrontation with the enemy and expect to win the war. So, Cao Cao cooked up a plan. He sent a unit to sneak into Yuan Shao's camp to set fire to every one of his 10,000 carriages loaded with grain supplies. A shortage of food drove Yuan Shao's army to despair. As they turned desperate, frustrated, and lost their fighting spirit, Cao Cao pounced on the chance to wage an all-out attack, dealing Yuan Shao's army the final blow.

New Spin on Funds

> **Time to sell**
> - Increasingly lackluster results
> - Mission accomplished
> - Set a limit for losses
> - Emergency cash needed
> - Unanticipated changes in the size of the fund

Time to sell

Volatile markets often send newbie investors reeling and into a bind as to whether to hold or sell their funds. The decision may not be such a nerve-wracking one if you borrow the military stratagem of "raking the fire from under the pot." What might have looked like an easy win for Cao Cao actually took a lot of smarts on his part. Investors should take a leaf out of Cao Cao's book. Do not panic and rush to redeem funds, or kill the hen that lays the golden eggs when you see a dip in prices after a sharp rise. For all you know, it may just be a short-term downward adjustment.

There is a market theory that an investor can bet on only a 25 percent probability of making a correct decision in a fund redemption. That is because its net asset value will likely sag by 50 percent after that, or rise by the same percentage when you re-enter the market. Simply put, one stands only a 25 percent chance of making the right redemption move.

So ask yourself: do I really have no choice but to make a redemption? This will help you make the right decision. You should seriously consider a redemption only if you encounter any of the five fund investment situations below.

Increasingly lackluster results. A fund may post spectacular net growth in performance in a year, but never take that to indicate good results. Likewise, a loss in net asset value does not make the fund an undesirable one. Only comparisons between funds of the same types or benchmarks for results can truly tell you whether a fund is producing good results or not. Long-term performance results of more than three years are the best and most reliable references. Do not redeem a fund due to a less than impressive spike.

Mission accomplished. All investors have different targets and goals. Some are preparing for retirement or building education funds for their children. Others are hoping to make enough to buy their dream homes or cars one day. Then, there are those who want to prevent their assets from depreciating, but do not expect any high rate of return from their investments. Whatever the case, an investor should expect a certain rate of return and risk. Once his or her goals are met, he or she can then proceed to consider making a redemption, and collect the returns.

Set a limit for losses. Profits and losses in investment are unpredictable. Nonetheless, it is always advisable to set a limit for losses. Regardless of whether or not you have achieved your goal, redeem your fund once your losses rise to a certain level. Decisiveness is key. For example, plan in advance, and make a conscious decision to withdraw from a fund the moment it slumps 20 percent. Never set a loss limit and not stick to it. Holding onto the thought that "prices may just rebound" will likely cause more grievous damage.

Emergency cash needed. We generally advise investors to create a fund portfolio that includes a currency fund or funds that are more fluid in nature. Ideally, the investment sum should be equivalent to a household's living expenses for six months to preempt the need for huge redemptions. However, profit will have to be discounted. When an emergency need arises, it is best to pick funds with the highest rates of return for redemption so that you can maintain the original portfolio ratio as much as possible.

Unanticipated changes in the size of the fund. When a fund that has been around for a reasonable period suddenly and radically expands or shrinks in size, find out the reason for it. A profit-taking opportunity may attract a flush of investment capital, and trigger an excessive rise. That could undercut the profit margin of genuine investors. In the case of a sudden reduction in fund size, institutional investors may be seeking redemptions to satisfy their cash-flow requirements or brace for a major turn in market events. So, once you are confronted with an abnormal change in fund size, redemption is a decision that you must consider.

Stratagem 20

Fish in Murky Waters (浑水摸鱼)

Fish for Bargains in Troubled Times

Origin of the Stratagem

The Chinese proverb "fish in murky waters" refers to a surprise catch in murky water while the fish in there are disoriented. It also refers to the military strategy of seizing the chance to trounce a foe when it is in a state of confusion.

A well-known example is the manner in which Wang Hui manipulated conflicts between the Qi Dan senior army generals to promote further discord and internal dissent among the Qi Dan people in the territory up north. With their forces weakened, the Tang army took the opportunity to wage a fierce attack to bring down the Qi Dan army.

New Spin on Funds

Dare to be different
Contrarian examples

Dare to be different

Today, the Chinese proverb "fish in murky water" has been given a modern spin to mean fish for bargains in times of crisis. The idea is, clear water makes fishing easy, but huge bargains are aplenty as well in muddy pools. So, if an astute buyer can make a killing on seasonal discounts, an adroit investor can also grab the opportunity to get ahead in a floundering market.

However, many trappings and dangers lurk in an investment market that operates in a capricious environment. It is like a war zone. To see gains over the long term, you cannot afford to let up in your investment efforts. Sometimes, it even requires you to have the courage to make a contrarian move. Capitalize on chaotic circumstances to enter the market, and make a tiny profit. You will then be truly living up to the investment adage of fishing for bargains in murky waters.

A plunging market makes most investors lose heart and confidence, but sometimes it presents a rare buying opportunity. By contrast, "the shoeshine boy theory" calls for caution when a market is too popular for its own good, and shoeshine boys without any investment experience are giving you tips on what stocks to buy!

Contrarian examples

The early part of 2007 saw markets extending their explosive trail. The wealth of money-making opportunities that were magnified several times stoked the flame of investors' passion for getting into the market. Record numbers of new stock market account registrations became a hot news topic. The A-share market registered more than 300,000 new account holders each day, with retailers being the most active in trading. However, their enthusiasm clearly took a bashing following a baptism by fire, in the form of a major market fallout in May and June. By the middle of July, the number of new A-share account registrations had swung below 70,000 per day.

However, it proved to be a short-term chance for bottom-fishing. From then right up till the end of October, the SSE Index ascended from roughly 3,800 points to break above 6,000 points.

A contrarian move is not purely about going against the current market trend. The investment scope of a fund and the question of sustainability both play a huge part in the success or failure of a contrarian move. Overall economic growth is hardly representative of the future performance of a stock. Thus, an investor must scrutinize a company's revenues, operations, gains, shareholder equities, and so on. All this is often difficult for the average investor to grasp, which therefore makes buying funds at low prices a reasonable option. However, the average investor often makes the common mistake of buying high rather than low in a fund investment. Funds launched at a time when the markets are in the doldrums have more cash to build their positions at lower costs, fostering more outstanding future results. Besides, it is also a good time to test the downward line resistance of a fund. A fund that has weathered many a storm and crisis will not only help investors to make extraordinary profits when the times are good, but it will also be able to withstand the pressures of market freefalls to continue to deliver the goods.

Funds customarily invest in several stocks to buffer themselves against the risk of a fall in any of the stocks. Therefore, a fund is generally better able to fight off a market meltdown than a stock. The credit also goes partially to a fund manager's wisdom in picking the right stocks and investment opportunities. Compiled data reports of the market downturn from the middle of 2004 to the end of 2005 reveal funds falling at a relatively small rate. Some funds were even able to fend off the risk of getting sucked into the downward spiral. Most impressive of all was their ability to shine through with spectacular returns. This is a lesson that it is not impossible to catch a big fish in murky waters!

Stratagem 21

Shed Your Skin Like the Golden Cicada (金蝉脱壳)

Separate Good Funds from the Bad

Origin of the Stratagem

"Shed your skin like the golden cicada" literally refers to the cicada morphing and molting in winter, leaving behind its shell on a tree branch.

History has recorded numerous successes of this military tactic. The most well known had to be Shu-Han Chancellor Zhuge Liang's "final act." During the Warring States Period, he led an army to Qi Mountain six times. Eventually, he fell sick from exhaustion and passed away in an army base in Wuzhangyuan or Wu Zhang Plains, Shaanxi Province. Before he died, Zhuge Liang told his deputy Jiang Wei not to leak news of his imminent death for fear

113

that the Wei army would take the chance to cut off the weakened Shu army's return route to Hanzhong. He also wanted artisans to carve a life-size wooden statue of him for his soldiers to dress up in his clothes before sitting it upright in a carriage and taking it with them on a charge against the Wei army.

When the Wei soldiers saw the Shu army approaching and Zhuge Liang's silhouette in the carriage from a distance, no one dared to make any aggressive move. Wei General Sima Yi even suspected Zhuge Liang of laying another devious trap for him, so he ordered his men to hold back, and keep a close watch on the Shu army's movements. While Sima Yi and his men were busy making a retreat, Jiang Wei instructed his main army unit to move out of the area and back to Hanzhong in double quick time. By the time Sima Yi got wind of Zhuge Liang's demise, it was too late for his men to catch up with the Shu troops.

New Spin on Funds

Steer clear of undesirable funds
• Investigate the finer details • Take note of shareholder changes
Fund managers make a difference
Dividends for better or worse

Steer clear of undesirable funds

It is a disgrace to flee because of cold feet, but honorable to beat a retreat when the situation calls for it. Zhuge Liang had to carry the weight of that, and design a game plan for his soldiers' retreat even before his own demise.

In investment terms, a fund manager has to know how to stay away from undesirable funds. However, in reality we have an increasing number of people working as fund managers but few who are fully prepared for the job. Getting stuck with an undesirable fund is no laughing matter. It could take a tremendous amount of time and money to wiggle out of it. The handling fees for buying and selling an open-end fund are 2 percent. That adds up to quite a large sum following several transactions. Coupled with that, buy and sell transactions take numerous working days to confirm and finalize.

Investigate the finer details. So, how best to steer clear of undesirable funds? Performance ranking provides the most direct insight. Apart from relying on the most obvious barometers, you also need to be astute enough to read between the lines within a short time. These finer details often make a qualitative impact on the performance of the funds, the level of stability in shareholding ownership, the sustainability of an investment research team, sales and marketing strategies, and so forth. They are factors to be considered as you plot your purchases or sales.

Take note of shareholder changes. Any changes in shareholders will likely bring about a change in investment strategy. Shareholder changes are not uncommon. Some fund companies even change their key shareholders frequently. There are two main situations: changes in key shareholders, and changes in secondary shareholders. Changes in secondary shareholders make a minimal impact on the investment performance of a fund company. Changes in the board of directors usually do not rock the stability of the management or the investment strategy. Changes in key shareholders, however, may affect a company in more ways than one, the evidence of which will gradually appear in the investment results over time.

Some fund companies initiate changes in shareholders to inject new blood. Older companies in search of a new lease of life often do so by attracting foreign shareholders. The tide of change begins with the revamp of the investment research system, the introduction of foreign know-how and manpower resource support, and much more. They are actions taken to lift the overall investment level of the company. Sale auctions or debt-swaps are sometimes used to push through shareholder changes when the original shareholders run into a liquidity crunch, or in the case of some strategic shakeups.

Currently, an individual is not allowed to sit on the board of more than one fund company. It is a check and balance against board member disputes over financial, personnel, strategic, and investment matters, particularly those pertaining to losses. But ironically, board disputes tend to break out in companies that are rolling in robust profits.

Fund managers make a difference

Changes in fund managers may affect the performance of funds. MorningStar China reported notices of changes in fund managers for 130 funds in 2006, 104 of which were due to resignations, and accounted for 33.8 percent of the total changes. Changes in fund managers have become even more rampant since 2007. A horde of fund managers have switched to the private equity business while others were forced to quit as they failed to cut it in the grueling business and ruthless competition.

The investment strategy of a fund essentially has to play by a set of stringent rules and regulations. But a fund manager always puts the stamp of his or her personal style on the funds that he or she is responsible for. That is especially true of celebrated fund managers who consistently produce spectacular results. A change in fund managers is not necessarily a bad thing, or one that will cause a fund to go downhill. However, if the scope of change is so large as to include the investment chief officer, core research officers, and so forth, it may reverberate through the entire system. Then, you had better brace for potential changes in the investment style.

Dividends for better or worse

An overly aggressive sales and marketing tactic may also kill off a potential money spinner. A proportionately large dividend may be inappropriate sometimes; for example, when the market is rising rapidly. Investors cashing in on dividends run the risk of missing out on a potential investment. In this case, dividend reinvestment is the way to go. Do not build your position in funds either when prices are on the rise, as you will incur higher costs and hurt your investment results instead. China International Finance Company Limited's 2007 statistical report shows more than 20 fund companies gave out proportionately large dividends. Within a month of the dividend payouts, most of the funds that recorded sterling performances previously had seen an 18.64 percent drop in performance on average compared to other funds in the same period, as well as a drastic fall in performance compared to the indices in the corresponding period. Thus, the fund investors who viewed the proportionately large dividends as a good way to make a fast buck would regret their decisions.

Stratagem 22

Shut the Door to Catch the Thief
(关门抓贼)

Keep Small-Cap Funds Within Your Grasp

Origin of the Stratagem

During the late Warring States Period, the Qin State attempted to annex the Zhao State in Changping, but it was unable to break through Zhao General Lian Po's tough line of defense in the four-month-long battle to get to the moat. The king of Qin decided to take Prime Minister Fan Sui's advice to poison the mind of the king of Zhao against Lian Po, so that the latter would be removed from the battlefield, and be replaced by Zhao Kuo, a war advocate.

Qin General Bai Qi deliberately fed Zhao Kuo with a few minor victories to make him complacent. As expected, Zhao Kuo became overconfident, and led a 400,000-strong army to try to

119

overpower the Qin troops. The Qin army decided to set a trap by pretending to have been brought down to its knees. As they backed off, another battalion of Qin soldiers was instructed to close in on Zhao Kuo's forces. Unaware of the situation, Zhao Kuo led a large force after the Qin soldiers. Only when he reached the Qin fortress did he realize he had been cornered. By then, it was too late. The Qin army had taken the chance to seize control of the Zhao camp, and cut off all its food supplies.

After being under siege for 46 days, and going without food, the Zhao soldiers resorted to killing and eating one another. Zhao Kuo died from an arrow wound. All his soldiers were wiped out by Bao Qi. The war went down in history as the Battle of Changqing.

New Spin on Funds

Size matters
• Small is good
• Big works too, sometimes
Clues from the markets

Size matters

"Shut the door to catch the thief" refers to the act of sealing off an enemy's escape route before the final massacre. According to the Chinese military stratagem, the act is motivated chiefly by the fear that an enemy will fall into another adversary's hands, rather than the need to cut off an enemy's escape.

Many people often bear the same investment mindset. They are concerned about who their fund managers are, much as an army commander is concerned about who his counterpart is, or who he is up against at the enemy's camp. Investors also always keep their ears cocked for the promotion of new funds, just as a soldier will stay attuned to an enemy's drumbeats, and calls for an attack. Despite all their alertness, investors tend to overlook the size of a fund, which is critical to their investments; not unlike the need of an army general to find out the number of his enemy's troops.

Small is good. The size of a share-based fund has a definite impact on its results. If the size of a fund expands to, let's say, tens of billions of *renminbi*, way beyond the average of its market peers, it will take a toll on its investment strategy, as well as its performance. That was the reason several funds limited the size of their sales between 2006 and 2007, as instructed by the Supervisory Administration Commission in its attempt to curb an irrational market frenzy and overzealous investment strategies.

There is endless market data to attest to the ability of small-sized and medium-sized funds to deliver better results than large or extremely large funds. The Chinese have a saying that a small boat is able to turn faster than a big one. The logical reasoning rings true for small-sized funds as well. Being small enables them to be nimble, to adjust their positions and holdings, and to lock in profits promptly as they move in tandem with stocks that are in favor at the time. Small-sized funds usually hold top billings in annual rankings.

In the first half of 2007, several small-sized funds, usually considered the underdogs, surprised everyone by overtaking their bigger and more prominent counterparts in performance. Subsequently, several mega-sized funds had to undergo a cycle and the process of downsizing. Bulk redemptions bogged many of these funds down, and hurt their net asset value.

Big works too, sometimes. Small is good, but the size of a fund should not be so small as to undermine the fund's ability to avert risk. The size of a fund should also evolve in tandem with market developments. In the past, a fund worth below RMB1 billion was classified as a small-sized fund, but with the likes of large-cap state-owned enterprises making their way into the A-share market, the liquid stockholding of the stock exchanges has been climbing steadily. That is a clear sign of changing times, which should also call for a change or an "upgrade" in the definition of "small."

Clues from the markets

Size matters, and investors are always anxious to find out the size of a fund. But they are convinced that they will only get to know about it after the completion of the launch. That is not true. Anyone can make a good guess by tracking the market's performance, and where it stands in relation to funds that have been launched only recently. If the market is on a rally, investors should avoid the latest fund debutant as it will probably carry an inflated price tag. The wisest move for any investor at this time is to put his or her money with a reliable old fund.

Practical tips

The "small-cap" funds mentioned in this book refer to small-sized funds, although "small-cap" is commonly used to refer to funds that specialize in penny stocks in fairly fixed, small-sized, medium-sized, and emerging growth markets, or shares with fixed liquidity. Overseas small-cap funds tend to close the door on further subscriptions once they balloon to a certain size, as they strive to maintain a consistent operating style and protect investors' interests.

The words "small cap" may appear in the name of a fund, but it does not necessarily mean that it is fully vested in small-cap shares of small market value. The same goes for funds that carry the words "large cap" in their names. They may not be completely vested in big-cap stocks of large market value. So, investors must always stay alert to such discrepancies to avoid making the wrong investment choices.

Stratagem 23

Befriend a Distant Enemy to Attack One Nearby
(远交近攻)

Stick to the Familiar

Origin of the Stratagem

The last few years of the Warring States Period were marked by a struggle for domination among seven powerful players. Under the stewardship of Statesman Shang Yang, the Qin State extended its power and influence most rapidly. Qin Zhaowang began plotting to swallow up the other six states to dominate the Central Plains.

In 270 BC, Qin Zhaowang was preparing to annex the Qi State when Fan Sui proffered the strategy of "befriending a distant enemy to attack one nearby." In a bid to stop the Qin State from attacking the Qi State, he warned Qin Zhaowang of the Qi State's formidable power and remote position from the Qin State. The Qin army would have to cut through the Han State and Wei State to get to the Qi State. If too small a force was sent, chances of victory would be slim. Even if a big force was sent, it would still be impossible to usurp the Qi territory. Fan Sui suggested moving in on the neighboring Han State and Wei State first before taking it progressively from there. To prevent the Qi State from closing ranks with the Han State and the Wei State, Qin Zhaowang sent an envoy to form an alliance with the Qi State.

For more than four decades, Emperor Qin Shihuang maintained a policy of "befriend a distant enemy to attack one nearby." He established friendly diplomatic relations with the Qi State and the Chu State, and then conquered the Han State and the Wei State before invading the Zhao State and the Yan State. Having unified the north, Qin Shihuang proceeded to crush the Chu State, and stabilized the south before taking the Qi State. After a decade of war, Qin Shihuang's hope of unifying China finally came to fruition.

New Spin on Funds

| Learn from Warren Buffett |
| Get familiar with fund companies and products |
| Funds on and off the radar |

Learn from Warren Buffett

Investment guru Warren Buffett has said he only invests in businesses that he understands. His philosophy may seem uncompromising, but even as he turned his back on the dotcom boom in the late 1990s and early 2000s, as well as real estate in China since 2003, he remains the most revered investment guru in the world.

Some people treat fund investments like stock speculation. They snap up advertized funds that claim to have recorded "multiple jumps in the rate of return from last year." Some people actually trade in whatever paltry savings they have to buy in and out of different funds. Like travelers who have caught wanderlust, these investors, bored with the same scenes and investments, are always seeking greener pastures or more promising yields.

Such a skewed investment concept or habit must be corrected, or even be avoided, at all costs. Instead, stick faithfully to familiar fund products, fund managers, and fund companies. That is the right thing to do. Familiarity builds trust, and trust generates returns as well as minimizes risk. After all, to let a complete stranger or a totally unfamiliar company manage one's money can be somewhat unsettling.

Get familiar with fund companies and products

We can borrow an idea or two from seasoned stock investors, like those in Shanghai or Shenzhen who are always focused purely on local companies, and completely ignore companies from other regions or overseas. They routinely call up the secretaries of company directors to be sure that they do not miss out on the chance to attend any shareholders' meetings. They cherish every nugget of information they can get hold of, from the state of the company management, products, and asset restructuring, to historical performances of funds. Making a conscientious effort to understand these companies assures the investors of reasonably stable returns in the long run.

Funds on and off the radar

Funds abound. There are those that do not appear in any listing or get any billing at all, and those that constantly make it to the list. A smart investor will invest in companies or products that he or she is familiar with, and those that rank higher in billboard listings. The companies that one is most familiar with are usually those closest to one geographically, or they are most likely to be local companies. Local fund companies tend to receive more local media exposure in the newspapers, on radio, on television, and in investment seminars. These companies may also organize company tours for investors. Not unlike interpersonal relationships, nothing builds a sense of trust better than face-to-face interaction. All this helps local investors strengthen their ties with the fund companies.

The saying "befriending a distant enemy to attack one nearby" is not just a warfare tactic, but also a sophisticated political strategy. The Chinese have another saying: "In a forbidding situation, gain by proximity and lose by distance." It means in case of geographical constraints or obstacles, attack the nearest enemies before you cross their territories to assault the ones farther afield. The moral of the story for fund investors is, they must keep a sharp eye on unfamiliar but geographically close companies, but choose familiar and geographically close companies to invest in.

Practical tip

Up until 2008, there was a total of 61 fund management companies in mainland China. There were 29 of them in Shanghai, 18 in Shenzhen, 7 in Beijing, 3 in Guangzhou, 2 in Chongqing, and 1 each in Nanning and Tianjin.

Stratagem 24

Borrow the Road to Conquer Guo (假道伐虢)

Trade Online to Increase Your Spread and Winnings

Origin of the Stratagem

During the Spring–Autumn Period, the Jin State wanted to annex two small neighboring states, the Yu State and the Guo State, but it knew the two were allies and would come to each other's rescue if attacked. To achieve its mission, the Jin State created a smokescreen by showering the Yu State with numerous gifts, before asking the Yu State to allow the Jin army to cut through its territory to get to the Guo State, and save it from trouble. Convinced, the Yu State acceded to the request. That allowed General Ban Shi to lead troops to annex the Guo State. On his way back, Ban Shi stationed his army on the outskirts of Yu, before launching a sneak attack on it a few days later while the king of Yu was out on a hunting expedition. Needless to say, the helpless and isolated Yu State quickly collapsed.

New Spin on Funds

The chink in the armor
Get online
• Discount privileges
• Efficiency in capital allocation
• The impact of bank cards
To each his or her own

The chink in the armor

The story about the States of Yu and Guo shows that a seemingly formidable alliance always has a chink in the armor, and all you need to do is look carefully to find it. You may apply the same skill to fund investment.

Just recently, we had a client who griped about new funds being launched one after another so quickly that he had difficulty keeping up with them. Very often, he had only a day to react. He then went on to describe his *modus operandi*. He would make appointments with other banks for his cash withdrawals before taking a bagful of cash to the fund distributors so that he could open accounts and apply for subscription. He would go on to do the reverse for making redemptions. No wonder he could not keep up with all the launches.

Get online

Our suggestion to this particular investor, and all other investors, is to consider the convenience of online transactions. Banks and many fund companies have set up online transaction platforms on their Web sites for fund application, subscription, and redemption.

This simplifies the fund investment procedures, and saves time. Online charges for handling fees also tend to be 40 percent to 60 percent lower than offline charges. For example, an over-the-counter transaction of a US$14,286 fund charges a subscription fee of 1.5 percent or US$211, while an online transaction charges only 0.6 percent. That is a difference of nearly US$129.

With online transactions, fund application and subscription is a breeze. All you need to do is get online, click the mouse, and submit your application. It totally frees you from the hassle of having to lug your cash around, or stand in long lines at the bank. However, do note that banks and fund companies operate online transactions quite differently.

Discount privileges. Online fund transactions with banks are regarded as indirect sales, as banks are sales agents for fund companies. Always bear that in mind when you make your online and offline fund transactions with banks. Banks have to negotiate with fund companies to determine the discount policies for different funds. Each fund comes with a unique discount policy. A bank may carry many funds, but it does not have a blanket discount policy for all the funds. So, investors must always check before applying for any fund subscriptions whether they are entitled to any discount privileges.

Online transactions with fund companies come under direct sales, and fund companies offer discounts only for their own funds. The discounts vary. Sometimes, a sales agent or fund distributor may not offer any discount for a fund, but the fund company may offer a discount for online transactions. The reverse may also occur.

Efficiency in capital allocation. As fund companies engage in direct sales online, they are generally more efficient in capital allocation.

For example, an investor making an online share-based fund redemption or a bond fund redemption directly with a fund company will see the transaction come through in T+3 or T+1 respectively; T+3 is the shorthand for trade date plus three days, and T+1 means trade date plus one day. They both mean that when you buy a security, your payment must be received by your brokerage firm no later than three and one business days respectively, after the trade is executed. When you sell a security, you must also deliver to your brokerage firm your securities certificate no later than three and one business days respectively, after the sale.

Online fund transactions with banks involve an extra layer of work. Fund companies have to assign the capital allocation to the banks for it to be relayed to the clients. Fund redemption at banks also takes longer; T+5 for share-based funds, and T+2 for bond funds.

If you are switching funds under the same fund company, an online transaction with a fund company works more efficiently. At the same time, you get to enjoy a discount in transfer fees. With a bank, the switching of funds can only be done if the bank is also the sales agent of the fund you want to transfer to. A bank may not necessarily carry every product of a fund company. It may not offer you a discount in transfer fees either.

The impact of bank cards. Bank cards normally divide assets into various classes. A card holding more than US$71,429 in assets is entitled to VIP privileges, and much more.

If you invest in a fund through a bank, the value of the fund will be included as part of your assets in the card. It will not jeopardize the class and status of your card. However, if you buy a fund online from a fund company directly, money will be deducted from your bank card, thus affecting its value. This is a loss to some bank card holders who hope to enjoy VIP services. But once you become a direct client of a fund company, you will also receive professional services and VIP treatments that are different from what a regular client gets. You win some, and you lose some.

To each his or her own

Buying from banks has an advantage, in that a bank is often the sales agent of numerous funds; sometimes as many as 100. Investors are spoiled for choice, and can choose whatever combinations of funds they wish to create multiple portfolios on the banking platform. If variety matters more than capital efficiency to you, online transactions with banks is the way to go. However, diehard fund investors are bound to find direct online transactions with fund companies more appealing.

Practical tips

Eight major advantages of HSBC Jintrust "e fund" electronic trading

1. **Safe transactions**

   Both the hardware and software of the electronic trading system are safely guarded by multiple data passwords. Even if a password is stolen, no one is able to move a person's fund assets to another person's bank account.

2. **Special discounts on fees**

   Front-end subscription fee discount rate of as much as 60 percent.

3. **24-hour trading**

   24/7 trading, at any time and place.

4. **Speedy transaction**

   Less time is needed to complete the redemption and transaction process. It usually takes one to two working days less than banks and brokerages.

5. **Simple and convenient operating system**

   You can open an account and make a transaction or an enquiry in a matter of minutes.

6. **Easy and convenient payment system**

   Accept various types of bank cards for the convenience of capital management.

7. **Complete package**

   The online system is fully equipped to facilitate a host of functions, from regular fund trading activities, online payments, and redemption, to custodian changes.

8. **Flexible regular fixed investment**

   Less time and effort is required when you go online to create a regular fixed-investment account, as well as make changes to payment dates and deductible sums.

Stratagem 25

Replace Beams with Rotten Timber (偷梁換柱)

Seek Out Alternative Investment Choices

Origin of the Stratagem

Emperor Qin Shihuang had an older son named Fu Su, and a younger boy name Hu Hai. Fu Su had forged a major political coalition with Meng Tian, and Hu Hai had done the same with Zhao Gao. The two brothers had been eyeing to usurp the throne for a long time. Qin Shihuang had intended to make Fu Su his successor. But upon his death, his letter of decree was stolen by Zhao Gao.

Zhao Gao then went on to warn Premier Li Si that his position would be severely threatened if Fu Su was crowned emperor upon his return to the imperial court from the southern territory with

General Meng Tian. Feeling insecure, Li Si decided to work with Zhao Gao to fake an edict sentencing both Fu Su and Meng Tian to death. However, the coronation of the hapless and useless Hu Hai as king heralded the decline and eventual demise of the Qin Dynasty.

New Spin on Funds

Use funds to cover a repertoire of products
• Commodities shine
• Bond attraction
• Take it from the indices
• Guaranteed returns for the asset-conscious
• Spare change for currency fund
• Fund of funds (FoF)
Building bridges

Use funds to cover a repertoire of products

In essence, "replace beams with rotten timber" is about faking something to bring about a qualitative and concrete change. It is an indirect but effective shortcut to make an extensive impact strategically.

Back to the fund market, the voluminous variety of investment products can make investors' heads swim. Just ferreting through copious pages of intricate and complicated information alone to choose the best investment opportunities can become a seemingly insurmountable task. This is evident from how several financial-oriented Web sites have evolved. A Web site that used to cover purely stocks has been expanding incessantly to include bonds, foreign currencies, commodities, insurance, gold, warrants, real estate, and several other products. Instead of pulling your hair out over the barrage of information, you may want to consider using funds as a bridge to invest in various markets.

Commodities shine. Early 2006 saw the prices of nonferrous metals, including gold, escalating to great heights in the commodity futures markets and the cash markets worldwide. Yet, an average individual investor has no way or avenue to counter-bid the trading of nonferrous metals. Neither is there a reason for him or her to buy up any gold bullion to stash away at home. However, any investor with an incisive mind will notice that many funds have been accumulating holdings in nonferrous metals and gold-related stocks. Therefore, you will enjoy a share of the stupendous returns if you invest in those stocks or funds. Simply holding different kinds of funds is another way to partake in the investment profits of different markets. There is no need for you to get personally involved in each and every market.

Bond attraction. As the name suggests, bond funds specialize in bonds, and they run the gamut, from government bonds, financial bonds, and corporate bonds, to convertible bonds. Bonds provide investors with fixed returns, and principal payment at maturity. The risk incurred is lower than stocks. Therefore, bond funds are more stable and less risky than share-based funds. But you still need to have sound professional knowledge of the host of bond products to make good investments. Bonds vary in maturity periods, fixed or floating interest rates, and purchase prices, whether they are sold at face value, or at discount rates, or at premium rates. Different types of bonds are also awarded different credit ratings. Prices fluctuate according to changes in the discount rates. In the case of convertible bonds, their convertibility to stocks upon maturity is tightly linked to the swap rate ratio and stock prices.

Certified treasury bonds or T-bonds are harder to cash out of, and early redemption may lead to a severe penalty in interest rates. However, you may stand to gain indirectly from this in many ways. Since you are in it for the long haul, you might as well explore the treasury issuance market for further investment opportunities, or get into the interbank market to invest in financial bonds that offer higher interest rates. You can make repurchases, and enjoy the privileges of an institutional investor in raising capital for your subscription of new shares, and in earning interest from zero-risk reverse repurchases. The cash assets of your fund investment are placed with the custodian bank, thus allowing you to enjoy the same interest rates as current account holders in the industry. These interest rates are much higher than the taxable interest rates of current account holders for residents and corporations. On top of all that, subscription and redemption are exempt from stamp duty. Dividends are also tax exempted. All in all, it is a low-cost exercise to invest in bonds through funds.

Take it from the indices. Some people depend on share-based funds to tap returns from the stock markets. As their knowledge and understanding of the markets deepens, many aspire to invest directly in the indices but find them impossible to get a hold of due to capital constraints and the highly specialized nature of the business. Index-linked funds are the solution to this problem. An index-linked fund adopts a passive mode of investment by modeling itself on a particular index, following the benchmarks set by the index and buying all or a portion of the securities covered by a market index. The goal is to achieve the same level of returns as the index. When you are buying an index-linked fund, the emphasis is on picking the index you want rather than choosing the right fund manager. The fund manager is not required to put together a basket of stocks or manage or track the fund for you anymore. As his or her role diminishes, it will also help to shave the costs of index-linked funds considerably, such as the management fees and the commissions that you have to pay.

Guaranteed returns for the asset-conscious. Some investors may put greater value on creating a safety net for their assets than anything else. Share-based funds are definitely out of the question for them as these funds are as vulnerable to high risk as they are capable of reaping hefty profits. Market upheavals often lead to downward adjustments in interest rates that can prove to be too much for faint-hearted investors. An alternative is to put your money in the bank, or better still, invest it in guaranteed funds.

Such funds adhere to a set of guarantee clauses. Assurance is given to the investor that he or she will get back the principal and be paid the investment returns once he or she has held such a fund for a stipulated period. The clauses of guaranteed funds vary, and there are clauses for principal assurance, revenue assurance, dividend assurance, and such. Companies also tend to set different maturity periods for their products. Investors should also realize that the insurance will become void in the event of a redemption before the date of maturity. Bound by such clauses, guaranteed funds are predestined to have little room for revenue growth.

Spare change for currency fund. Any remaining cash that you have after putting aside money for your household expenses can be invested in a currency fund. It will be like a working asset in a current-savings account, whereby you earn interest that is almost as attractive as that of fixed deposits without having to pay any taxes on it. Any urgent need to redeem the fund can be handled quickly at the bank; $T+1$, or trade date plus one business day. Some innovative banks have even introduced credit cards for currency funds to allow investors to spend on credit, and effect an automatic redemption of their currency funds upon maturity.

Fund of funds (FoF). For the uninitiated, or inexperience market investors, or folks who are too busy to manage their investment portfolios, fund of funds could be the solution. Managers of such funds come up with different portfolios from hundreds and thousands of funds to help investors achieve their investment returns and goals more easily.

Building bridges

So, never underestimate the ability of funds to serve as a bridge to various markets, to break down barriers and monopolies, and to tap into the wealth of money-making opportunities within.

Stratagem 26

Point at the Mulberry but Curse the Locust Tree
(指桑骂槐)

A Different Kind of Close-End Fund

Origin of the Stratagem

During the Spring-Autumn Period, King He Lu of the Wu State read *The Art of War*, the famous book written by military strategist Sun Tzu, and was duly impressed. He then invited Sun Tzu to perform and demonstrate his skills in court. To test him, King He Lu sent 180 courtesans to take part in the performance. The girls did not take it seriously or pay much attention at first. But with great patience, Sun Tzu explained the drills, and iterated that any recalcitrant behavior would face military punishments.

During the actual exercise, the girls remained giggly, and failed to obey his commands. Sun Tzu kept his cool, and explained in detail once again the key exercise movements. After that, he asked the courtesans whether they understood his instructions. The girls responded with a loud yes in unison, but once again failed to respond to the cue when the drums were sounded. This time, the expression on Sun Tzu's face turned austere as he exclaimed: "If a general fails to clarify how the drill should be conducted, he is at fault. If the message has been clearly conveyed but the soldiers disobey the commands, the soldiers are at fault. Take the two team leaders away to be executed!"

As they were King He Lu's favorite courtesans, he pleaded on their behalf, but to no avail. Sun Tzu sent the courtesans to the guillotine as a warning to the others. The rest of the girls were so shaken and scared that when the drums sounded for the third time, the girls kept their focus and discipline in demonstrating the exercise. With a no-nonsense attitude, they completed the drills smoothly.

New Spin on Funds

Open-end funds versus close-end funds
• Size and holding period
• Determinants of fund prices
• Revenue streams
• Trading channels
• Management criteria and investment strategies
• Rationale of dividends
New variations of funds

Open-end funds versus close-end funds

Taking one or two persons to task to serve as a warning to the rest is a way of shaking up a system. Investors may sometimes debate the pros and cons of close-end funds and open-end funds. The argument may revolve around how close-end funds are able to grow faster, pay out more dividends, and are better bargains than open-end funds. However, they are completely missing the point. Close-end funds and open-end funds are as different as chalk and cheese. No comparison is possible.

Close-end funds in China began to take shape in the early 1990s. The capital market was still in its infancy; the market size was small, and the authorities were still putting the finishing touches to rules and regulations binding the industry. As market conditions grew more mature, the fund market introduced its first open-end fund in 2001. The structure of the product threw light on the distinct differences between open-end funds and close-end funds.

Size and holding period. On one hand, the size of a close-end fund is fixed and immutable. For example, a fund set at US$429 million at the launch will remain that size throughout its holding period of 20 years, and will not be allowed to accept new subscriptions and redemptions. On the other hand, the size of an open-end fund is dictated by market conditions at the launch, and investors are allowed to make subscriptions and redemptions at any time they wish. Hence, the size of an open-end fund is fluid.

Determinants of fund prices. Fundamentally, the prices of close-end funds, like stock prices, are determined by market supply and demand. In times of poor liquidity, the face value of close-end funds may drop way below their net asset value to result in a discount price. Meanwhile, discount prices do not exist in the open-end fund market as the unit price is equivalent to the net asset value.

Revenue streams. Due to the factors affecting prices, close-end funds derive their revenues mainly from differentials in buying and selling prices in the secondary markets. In the case of open-end funds, revenues are largely derived from the differentials in redemption prices and subscription prices. They make up the net value growth generated by the fund manager, depending on his or her ability.

Trading channels. Like stocks, close-end funds are brokered through securities houses, and their trading partners are other investors. As a result, transaction fees are relatively low. In the case of open-end funds, investors apply for subscription and redemption with fund companies, banks, and securities agents. Fund companies are their trading partners, and they charge relatively high handling fees.

Management criteria and investment strategies. Open-end funds always put aside a portion of cash to meet redemption requirements, and that can pose a management challenge. This feature is absent in close-end funds, which enables their fund managers to operate their assets at full capacity within a fixed scale and within a stable environment. Open-end funds are also subject to greater disclosure requirements with regard to information on investment portfolios and more.

Rationale of dividends. Dividends are distributed to investors after the actualization of investment revenues. Investors of open-end funds may choose dividend payouts or redemptions to take profits. Redemption is completely out of the question for investors of close-end funds. Faced with severely discounted prices in the secondary markets, a long-time close-end fund investor can only seek relief by collecting cash dividends.

According to transaction rules and regulations, a dividend is equal to the sum of the net asset value and the price of the fund ex-dividend. Dividends tend to drive the rate of discount prices higher in the short term. The rate of discount prices is the difference in ratio between net asset value and the price of the fund. For example, a close-end fund with a net asset value of US$1.30, and a price of US$1, claims to distribute a dividend of US$0.20. Before the dividend payout, the discount price rate stood at 23 percent (0.3 ÷ 1.3 percent). After ex-dividend, the net asset value changes to US$1.1, and the price of the fund will drop to US$0.80. The discount price rate will then reach 27 percent (0.3 ÷ 1.1 percent). Theoretically, dividends distribution of close-end funds is able to expand the rate of discount prices, which serves to bolster the allure of high-performing close-end funds.

New variations of funds

As markets develop, more creative spin-offs of open-end funds and close-end funds are making an appearance. Examples include listed-open funds or LOFs that are allowed to make transactions on the trading floors of stock exchanges; some innovative close-end funds can now even trade on a restricted basis.

China's capital market will become progressively more open. More innovative products will flood the market. They will become more diversified. Seemingly similar and yet essentially very different financial investment products will emerge in large numbers. They will be a definite challenge to investors who are inclined to make superficial comparisons about funds.

Practical tips

Close-end funds are listed on both the Shanghai Stock Exchange (SSE) and the Shenzhen Stock Exchange (SZSE). Close-end funds are called "Fund XX," while open-end funds are known as "XX Fund." Fund Kexiang and Fund Jinxin are examples of close-end funds. Every close-end fund in the SSE has a code starting with the digit "5." For instance, Fund Jinxin is 500011. Over at the SZSE, the codes for close-end funds begin with the digits "184." Hence, Fund Kexiang becomes 184713.

If an investor's aim is to invest only in close-end funds, and not in the A-share market, he or she can get securities brokers to help set up an individual fund transaction account for a fee of just RMB5 (US$0.71). You can even use the account to buy and sell bonds. For those investors who are already securities transaction account holders, there is no need for them to open separate fund transaction accounts. Each trading commission should not be more than 0.3 percent of the transaction sum, with RMB5 as the starting point. Handling fees are also based on the transacted amounts. The SSE and SZSE charge 0.0045 percent and 0.00975 percent respectively. There is also a securities management fee of 0.004 percent with stamp duty exempt.

Stratagem 27

Feign Ignorance to Bide Time
(假痴不癫)

A Smart Way to Understand MorningStar's Rankings

Origin of the Stratagem

During the Three Kingdoms Period, Cao Cao and Liu Bei got together to reminisce about past glories over some green plum wine.

One of the stories revolved around Liu Bei's deceptive act of madness when he harbored aspirations of building an empire for himself, which he succeeded in doing much later, adopting the imperial title of Liu Xuande. Before he became the founding emperor of Shu-Han in 221 AD, Liu Bei did not command a great deal of power, and had to live in Cao Cao's shadow. To hide his ability and bide his time, Liu Bei pretended to be ignorant of everything except tending to his vegetable farm and his resolution to be a farmer.

One day, Cao Cao invited him for a drink and a chat. In the midst of talking about heroes, Cao Cao suddenly declared: "You and I are the only heroes in the world!" In a moment of panic as he feared that Cao Cao might decide to kill him off, Liu Bei dropped the chopsticks in his hand. Just then, thunder struck. He immediately seized upon it as an excuse and a cover. He explained to Cao Cao he was cowering from the thunder, and called himself a useless man.

But in days to come, Liu Bei gradually broke loose from Cao Cao's grip, and became a power to be reckoned with. This eventually led to the emergence of The Three Kingdoms.

New Spin on Funds

Internet forums on rankings
MorningStar
• Fair comparisons   • Star reading
Unclear connection between ratings and performance
Approach MorningStar with care

Internet forums on rankings

The Chinese stratagem of "feigning ignorance to bide time" also implies striking only when one is armed with a full understanding of the situation.

Some popular questions posted on the message or bulletin boards of Internet forums concern whether there is a need to move swiftly to redeem funds when the going gets tough, or when MorningStar downgrades the ratings of certain funds. These questions are usually raised by newbie investors, who hope to draw on the insights of their more experienced counterparts. Yet, even as they do so, most of them have made up their minds about the funds they would buy or sell, or they would jump right into a deal the minute someone reinforces their opinions.

Investors should never act on the spur of the moment. Do not be swayed by smooth-talking salespeople into buying certain funds, or by fellow investors into bludgeoning and ditching certain funds. Basing your decisions on good reasoning and professional sensibility is paramount. As the saying goes, look before you leap.

Some people may be wise enough not to rely on the opinions of others in Internet forums to make their decisions, and proclaim that they decide their investment moves independently by consulting the MorningStar rankings. But relying on those rankings and ratings alone is not good enough either. The MorningStar ratings merely provide a starting point in helping you to make your choice. Bear in mind that many rating benchmarks are based on different criteria, lest you misjudge their actual purpose.

MorningStar

Fair comparisons. Let's say an investor has purchased a fund called Fund A. He started comparing the data of Fund A with those of the other funds each night after the net asset value was announced. After a few weeks of careful scrutiny, he discovered that the price of Fund A was accelerating slower than Fund B, and decided to bail out of Fund A immediately to cut his losses. That would be a mistake if the two funds did not belong to the same type or category of funds that warrant any comparisons. To quote MorningStar, compare an apple with an apple, not another fruit of a different type or category.

MorningStar categorizes funds according to investment portfolios. The categories comprise share-based funds, aggressive composite funds, conservative composite funds, regular bond funds, short-term bond funds, currency funds, and guaranteed funds. Different timelines are used to measure fund performance and risk-adjusted return, before funds are finally benchmarked into five classes.

There are different scenarios that we can easily observe. One, a share-based fund is likely to benefit more than a composite fund from a bull market. Two, comparisons are not possible between two composites funds if one is conservative and bond-oriented while the other is aggressive and share-oriented. Three, a share-oriented composite fund is likely to lag behind a conservative and bond-oriented fund if the industries that the share-oriented composite fund's blue-chip holdings are in have not reached their cyclical peaks.

Star reading. Some investors will shudder when they see the funds they are holding drop in standing on the MorningStar rankings from five stars to four stars, and then to three stars. As the pressure gets to them, they may decide to cut them loose.

MorningStar categorizes funds of the same types from big to small in star ratings according to their risk-adjusted return. The top 10 percent are awarded five-star ratings, the following 22.5 percent receive four-star ratings, the next 35 percent are studded with three stars, then two stars for the 22.5 percent that come after that, and finally one star for the remaining 10 percent.

Unclear connection between ratings and performance

There is no clear connection between the MorningStar ratings and the results or performance of funds. Therefore, the idea that you can simply use the MorningStar ratings to dictate your buying and selling decisions is completely flawed. The ratings are no projection of future results. They are only reflections of previous showings. High ratings merely demonstrate commendable performance in the past. They are no guarantee of great results in the future.

MorningStar ratings do not take into consideration every single piece of vital information related to the funds, such as changes in fund managers, fund expenditures, and investment portfolios. For various reasons, different types of funds may be awarded the same ratings, but a five-star fund may not bring in as much revenue as a four-star fund. Revenue is not the only barometer used by MorningStar. A fund that racks up average returns with minimum risk may sometimes receive top billing. Conversely, a high-performing and high-risk fund may be rated lowly. Under such circumstances, if its earnings were not part of the equation, it is critical for an investor to identify what else could be responsible for a drop in a fund's star ratings.

Generally speaking, the risk and return ratios of different types of assets tend to be proportionate over the long run. However, if we go by the investment period of a regular investor, the asset gains sometimes do not correspond with the risk involved. By and large, when interest rates drop, bond funds usually do better than share-based funds, and that has nothing to do with the ability of the fund managers.

Approach MorningStar with care

It is hard to explain away the mechanisms that make funds tick, or how practical MorningStar is as a measurement tool. It certainly is useful, to some extent. The outcome of its star ratings is, to a great measure, a reflection of the fund managers' investment management ability, and their ability to steer clear of unsavory market conditions and other elements that are beyond their control. So, use MorningStar as a reference guide by all means, but make sure you know how to read between the lines, and glean the details, and not just skim the surface.

Investment guru Warren Buffett has said investment is more about avoiding foolhardy strategies than following a few brilliant strategies. We could not agree with him more. A single mistake in buying or selling might not put a dent in the money that you have made so far, but it could mean a huge opportunity cost in other areas. The key is, therefore, to switch into low gear in investment and take time out to do your homework, before you make your next big move.

Stratagem 28

Lure the Enemy Onto the Roof and Remove the Ladder (上屋抽梯)

Know Your Investment Targets to Make Headway

Origin of the Stratagem

After the fall of the Qin Dynasty (221 BC–206 BC), the Chu State and the Han State were engaged in a power struggle. Liu Bang ordered his generals Han Xin and Zhang Er to lead a 20,000-strong elite force to attack Jingxing against Prince Zhao Xie, who was holed up there. It was a refuge provided by Xiang Yu. Forced into a corner, Prince Zhao Xie had no choice but to gear his 200,000-strong army up for war.

Meanwhile, Han Xin warned Zhang Er they were outnumbered more than tenfold by the enemy, and that it would be foolhardy to go head to head with them. To outfox them, Han Xin suggested splitting up the troops, and getting them to move in on the enemy from three different directions.

At the break of dawn, Han Xin led a company of 8,000 soldiers to Jingxing to battle it out with the Zhao army commanded by Chen Yu. Amid the fierce fighting, Han Xin suddenly ordered his men to feign defeat and beat a retreat. Chen Yu laughed at their cowardice, and set off in hot pursuit. Han Xin and his battalion backed all the way to the Mianyan riverbank to regroup with Zhang Er's 10,000 awaiting troops. Then, Han Xin told his soldiers: "We are wedged between the river and the enemy. We are cornered, and have no choice but to fight our way out." The soldiers responded to his call with inimitable courage, and were determined to fight to the end. The scene perturbed Chen Yu. He immediately urged his army to pull back.

As they approached their barracks, countless arrows shot from the camp rained upon them. Chen Yu and his men were shocked and befuddled as to why their own people were taking aim at them. Apparently, Han Xin had sent 2,000 snipers and commandos to slip into the Zhao army barracks and erect Han military flags all over the place. The Zhao army was coming under fire from the Han troops from both sides. Chen Yu was pulled from the back of his horse by Zhang Er, and killed in a single blow. Prince Zhao Xie was captured alive while his troops were completely wiped out.

New Spin on Funds

Define your own purpose for personal finance management
Analyze your needs and desires

Define your own purpose for personal finance management

The Chinese military stratagem "lure the enemy onto the roof, and remove the ladder" is all about tempting an enemy with a carrot. For such a strategy to work, a tool, such as a ladder, has to be used to accomplish the mission. The strategy has been effectively used since time immemorial for fighting do-or-die battles. It can also be employed to make winning and accurate fund investments. First, you have to define for yourself the purpose of investment finance. This may seem superfluous, but it is a profound exercise. Once you are able to determine the purpose, you will discover that the purpose determines the outcome.

If you do not have the foggiest idea of your own purpose for personal finance management, you are on shaky ground. You can hardly claim to have built a solid foundation for your dealings with your investment partners, your risk/return ratio, your investment holding period, a time frame for withdrawals, and an assessment outcome. Many investors like to ask for fund recommendations, or advice on when to make redemptions. This is a classic example of people not laying the necessary groundwork to help them achieve their goals.

Investors like to say they are buying funds to make money. That is true, but the better informed ones will say they are buying funds to fight inflation, or to make more than what savings interest rates are able to offer, or to profit from China's economic boom in the long run. These are all correct but fairly standard answers. Even as we live by those beliefs and are taking advantage of the situation, what exactly do they mean to us in life?

Analyze your needs and desires

Most people in the world need more money than they actually have, and are always in search of means to satisfy their endless needs with limited capital. People can actually come to grips with their needs and desires by categorizing them into short-term and long-term goals, as well as small and big desires. Financial planning and management is necessary to make all these dreams come true. For instance, a three-year savings plan to build the first US$75,000 installment for a home purchase, a US$150,000 education fund for the children 10 years down the road, a US$300,000 pension fund invested over a 30-year period to finance 40 years of retirement, an annual loan repayment of US$7,000, and annual traveling expenses of US$4,000. As you do your math, it should factor in inflationary rates and projected rates of investment returns to give you a rough idea and structure of what your investment finance plan should look like.

If the first installment for a home purchase is a large amount and has to be paid within a short period, you may want to invest in a share-based fund in a market where property and stocks are closely tied. Meanwhile, the education fund and retirement fund require investment products that are risk-resilient, and provide a stable income. Market gyrations make a negligible impact on long-term investments. Therefore, fixed-income investment funds are the best choices for building the education fund and retirement fund. Fixed-income investment also forces one to be disciplined in working toward one's goals.

Technically speaking, a young investor has time on his or her side, so he or she can afford to invest in funds that involve relatively high risk. Just before the funds come to maturity, the investor can transfer his or her investment into more stable products. You can achieve ultimate financial freedom by carefully plotting and perfecting a long-range plan. Do not expect luck to help you strike gold. That happens only one in a million times.

Once you are able to map out all the big and small goals in your life, and accomplish them one by one with the help of a comprehensive financial plan, you will not have to eke out a living, or worry about where your next meal is going to come from.

Hence, funds are there for you to make a conscious effort to plan and map out your goals in life, so as to achieve ultimate financial freedom. Know what is needed to get the job done. Be clear in your head about your wants and desires to know what apparatus or types of funds will help you best in realizing your dreams.

Stratagem 29

Tie Silk Blossoms to the Dead Tree (树上开花)

Suffer No Illusion When It Comes to the "Bubble"

Origin of the Stratagem

During the Three Kingdoms Period, Liu Bei took control of Jingzhou after the death of his brother, Liu Biao. When Cao Cao mobilized his troops down south, Liu Bei immediately moved his Jingzhou forces to defend Jiangling. In Dangyang, Cao Cao's troops confronted and defeated Liu Bei's army. Left with a meager cavalry of 30, Liu Bei's trusted deputy Zhang Fei had virtually no room to maneuver against Cao Cao's massive force.

Nevertheless, Zhang Fei remained calm and undeterred. Armed with a plan in mind, he ordered his cavalry to cut some branches in the woods, secure them to the backs of the horses, and ride the horses around the woods. Meanwhile, Zhang Fei rode with his long spear lying horizontally across his stallion, looking formidable as he stood on the Changban Bridge. When the enemy soldiers arrived, they were astounded by the scene of Zhang Fei standing alone on the bridge while flying dust fogged up the entire Jiaodong forest. Afraid that their enemies were lying in ambush in the woods, Cao Cao's soldiers halted their advance, and eventually beat a retreat.

By creating an illusion with the help of a small legion of soldiers, Zhang Fei managed to fend off Cao Cao's army so that Liu Bei and the Jingzhou forces could make a smooth escape.

New Spin on Funds

Profit-taking activities
Overnight success stories
A shift in investment style
Maintain a long-range focus

Profit-taking activities

The silk blossoms in the Chinese saying "tie silk blossoms to the dead tree" refer to Chinese fake flowers that are traditionally made out of silk. The stratagem uses an illusion that requires minimal effort to make a huge impact. Such a move is also commonly used in the fund market. For example, some media reports may mention a fund's continued ability to attract billions of *renminbi* in subscriptions despite recent spates of redemptions. It may sound impressive, but as you delve deeper you may discover that the fund is simply prey to speculative profit-taking rather than a genuine market darling.

Profit-taking is most likely to seep in when a fund consists of stocks that are suspended from trading due to shareholding changes or restructuring. Some institutions holding hefty sums of capital are likely to subscribe to the fund when trading activity is being suspended. They are waiting to lock in large profits when the prices of those stocks soar upon the resumption of trade. Consequently, genuine investors are frequently left with a thinner spread and some potential damage, while the fund gained only a momentary enlargement in size.

Henceforth, investors should not be irate when funds announce temporary halts in accepting huge blocks of subscriptions, as they are just trying to protect investors' interests. In other cases, funds may tolerate some profit-taking for certain diplomatic reasons, albeit with genuine investors being kept in the dark most of the time.

Overnight success stories

We have also heard of funds achieving overnight successes. Their meteoric rise often draws sighs of admiration, but investors should stay clear-eyed to the possibility that these funds may just be one-hit wonders.

There are many explanations for such windfalls. Share-based funds may enjoy sudden good fortunes due to a sharp rally in blue chips that the funds are heavy-weighted in, or a cyclical rise in the prices of obscure stocks held for a long period. Meanwhile, currency funds offloading different currency notes bought previously to cash in on the price differentials may register a short spike in revenue. Deploying a huge sum of capital to subscribe to a new large-cap stock may also cause the repurchase or repo rate in the stock exchange to surge. It is critical for investors to be able to tell whether all this is a sign of a long-term trend to come, or whether it is simply a fluke.

Generally speaking, the investment value of a share-based fund should be evaluated based on its results and performance over more than two years. The seven-day annualized yields of most currency funds are fairly similar, since investors are buying out of convenience rather than in hot pursuit of high returns.

A shift in investment style

Funds rarely shift in their investment style, but it can still potentially happen. It is therefore good to keep an eye out for it, in case an investment style digresses from the contractual agreement. For example, a fund is officially listed as a medium-yield and medium-risk product. But a fund manager may decide to be more aggressive in going after gains and making it onto the ranking list, thereby transforming the product into a high-yield and high-risk fund. This may confuse investors with regard to the risk/return feature of the fund, and cause them to shoulder unnecessary risk. Therefore, any investor shopping for products to buy should pay equal attention to the funds' investment returns, their risk/return features, as well as the level of disclosure in the contractual agreements.

Maintain a long-range focus

Investors may find it a challenge to sidestep all the landmines created by professional institutions. A flood of market information may interfere with their thoughts and cloud their judgment initially, but an illusion or a bubble can never last long. In no time, the true state of affairs will reveal itself. So, a long-term investment is the best policy. Do not give in to a moment's greed.

Stratagem 30

Switching from the Role of a Guest to that of a Host
(反客为主)

Exercise Owners' Rights

Origin of the Stratagem

"Switching from the role of a guest to that of a host" means switching to a proactive stance from a passive one to capitalize on the chance to initiate a strike.

During the Three Kingdoms Period, Yuan Shao and Han Fu were initially allies who worked hand in glove to annex Dong Zuo. When Yuan Shao was expanding his territory aggressively and faced a shortfall in grain supplies, his good old friend Han Fu would come to his rescue.

However, Yuan Shao knew that was not a long-term solution. So, he hatched a plan to wrestle management control of the grain storage warehouse in Yizhou from Han Fu's hands. First, he instigated Gongsun Zan to terrorize Yizhou, and sent a man to convince Han Fu to join him in fighting Gongsun Zan to prevent Yizhou from being taken away.

Even though Han Fu knew what Yuan Shao was up to, he had no option but to invite Yuan Shao and his troops to Yizhou. As a guest, Yuan Shao showed due deference to Han Fu. But in reality, he had started planting his men in every vital part of Yizhou to consolidate his position. Knowing that his guest was hijacking his position as the host, Han Fu fled Yizhou.

New Spin on Funds

An investor's onus
The rights of shareholders
Services offered by fund companies
• Customer phone lines and company Web sites
• Short message service (SMS)
• Professional opinions and analyses
• Financial planning services
• Face-to-face interaction
Register and flag your membership

An investor's onus

Every fund investor dreams of finding a good fund manager who can provide the best returns and service. Oftentimes, an investor pays for a fund and leaves a fund manager to take care of everything, hoping that it will work out just fine. If it doesn't work out, the investor may grumble about it, but he or she is actually to blame for not protecting his or her own rights.

It is common to hear investors complain that some fund companies provide lousy service, that they do not bother to issue statements or reports, that fund managers do not care to provide any after-sale service, or meet up with them to help clarify any questions or problems that they may have. But are the fund companies or managers to blame if you have not furnished them with your address or established a way for you to contact each other?

From a legal viewpoint, you are the rightful owner of your fund assets, while fund companies and banks are only responsible for managing and overseeing the assets. In fact, a fund holder is entitled to a tremendous number of rights.

The rights of shareholders

According to investment fund law in China, fund shareholders are entitled: to the returns made on investment; to request fund shareholders' general assembly meetings; to vote on items on the agenda at the fund shareholders' general assembly meetings; to sue the fund managers, or fund custodians, or the sales distributors of funds for any damages; and so on. Fund shareholders' general assembly meetings are similar to a company shareholders' general assembly meetings. As long as you fulfill the relevant criteria, you have the power to vote on many important issues, such as those relating to fund swaps, changes in fund managers or custodians, and premature termination of fund contracts. Every fund shareholder has a say over all those matters.

Services offered by fund companies

However, a shareholders' general assembly meeting is seldom called. Regular investors can usually exercise their rights by using the services that the fund companies have proffered them.

Customer phone lines and fund company Web sites. Making phone enquiries using the customer service lines or checking the fund company Web site enables investors to find out how their funds are doing in terms of their net asset value, operations, and more. They can also request free information materials, such as quarterly reports, annual reports, other special reports, and bulletins.

Short message service (SMS). Subscribing to the SMS platform provided by fund companies allows investors to keep tabs on such matters as dividends, new launches, distribution of funds, and discount privileges. Investors can also find out through the service—which is usually provided free—the weekly and monthly yields of funds.

Professional opinions and analyses. Investors are able to consult fund companies for their views on a full range of issues, like interest rate hikes, the implications of an overheating market, market trends, and market developments.

Financial planning services. You can also consult fund companies at any time about matters relating to the allocation of your children's education fund, whether you should buy a house or a car, whether you have built an ample nest egg for your retirement, and so forth.

Face-to-face interaction. Fund companies host various types of meetings with investors every year, often in the form of investment strategic reports meetings and events. They provide great opportunities for face-to-face interaction with fund managers, chief investment officers, and the senior management team.

Register and flag your membership

New investors usually buy their funds from banks, brokerages, and other sales agents. They do not have direct contact with the fund companies. Hence, the best way to ensure that you receive a more comprehensive service package is to register yourself on the fund companies' Web sites, or call the companies to confirm the registration of your personal details. Do not assume that once you have bought a fund, the fund company will know where to find you or how to contact you. Take it upon yourself to establish a direct link with the fund company.

Stratagem 31

Seductress at Work (美人计)

Are Star Managers for Real?

Origin of the Stratagem

Xi Shi was one of the renowned four great beauties of ancient China. She lived in the Spring-Autumn Period. King Gou Jian of the Yue State presented her to King Fu Chai of the Wu State to seduce him so that he would turn weak-willed and decadent. As Gou Jian would have it, Fu Chai spent day and night drinking and making merry. He began to lose all interest in state affairs. His chief minister Wu Zixu became worried, and urged Fu Chai to execute Xi Shi. But Fu Chai would not listen. Instead, he sentenced Wu Zixu to death. Shortly after, Gou Jian revealed his ulterior motive by sending an army to squash the Wu State and kill Fu Chai.

New Spin on Funds

Playing on appearance
The making of a celebrity fund manager
Division of labor
Investment research team composition and performance
• Attractive brand status and remuneration package
• Strong corporate culture and management
• Stability in share ownership and management
Professional ethics

Playing on appearance

Beautiful girls attract stares. Some are such head-turners that some people find it hard to tear their eyes away from them. Likewise, investors fall for the funds of celebrity fund managers. Even the most rational and sensible investors may succumb to their gloss and glitter.

It is a military tactic that you should make the enemy general your chief target if you are clearly outnumbered by his troops, and manipulate the enemy in spirit to browbeat him if he is a man of shrewdness. Unlike most of the other 36 stratagems that employ decoys to fool the foes, "seductress at work" is a unique stratagem in the sense that it manipulates the weakest foible of humankind to undermine an adversary. The stratagem involves emotional manipulation, and use of the halo effect; that is, to let an impression of a person or trait influence one's overall judgment of that person.

The making of a celebrity fund manager

It is common for investors to be drawn to funds run by celebrity fund managers, even if the fund managers are no seductresses. Celebrity fund managers build their credit on having scored excellent results and won numerous accolades in the past. That convinces investors that these celebrity fund managers will continue to churn out top-notch results, and turn a fund on its head to make its way up to the top spot in the ranking, regardless of market turbulence or how badly hit a fund has been. This is what we mean by the halo effect.

Apart from delivering exceptional results, a celebrity fund manager is also thrust into the limelight by the sleek packaging of a professional marketing team and media exposure. The outstanding work done by a fund research team is also, to a large extent, behind the success of a fund.

Division of labor

A fund company usually has various departments that include research, strategy, management, transaction, and evaluation. These departments work independently and coordinate with one another at the same time to keep the investment business well-oiled.

Then, there are the various committees. The investment committee holds regular meetings to discuss major issues pertaining to the investment business. The risk control committee follows the internal risk control system in supervising and regulating the investment process every step of the way, to sieve out and resolve all kinds of potential risks and ensure the operational security of fund assets. The chief compliance officer and the compliance and audit department are responsible for putting in place the legal framework to supervise fund investments. The fund managers, research officers, and trading officers work closely together to serve as checks and balances for one another in the investment management process.

In the process of creating stock investment portfolios, the investment research team has to read voraciously about all types of investment reports. Based on the research officers' field studies of public companies and a selection process based on the Ultimate Oscillator Index (UOI), stocks are separated into a preliminary pool and a premium pool. They are then tested successively on various complex mathematical models and data analysis systems to produce and formulate an investment portfolio. Then, the actual buying and selling, which is what regular investors are familiar with, comes into the picture. After every transaction, the portfolio continues to undergo assessment, adjustment, and analysis for its investment risk and objective before further projections are made.

A fund manager cannot possibly accomplish all these tasks single-handedly. A celebrity fund manager may leave the team and join another team, and gradually lose his or her Midas touch in the markets. This shows that even the best fund manager cannot afford to underestimate the contribution of his or her teammates. A well-respected fund manager once said he contributed 3 percent to 5 percent in personal impact to the success of his investment portfolio. Peter Lynch, a Wall Street investment expert, has also attributed his success in racking up brilliant results to the teamwork demonstrated by his highly skilled management team.

Thus, investors should focus on the investment research team supporting the fund manager rather than just bet on a certain fund manager. This may enable a fund to remain largely unaffected even with the departure of its manager.

Investment research team composition and performance

Several factors usually come together to determine the makeup and performance of an investment research team.

Attractive brand status and remuneration package. A good company brand and relatively high pay package attract top talent easily.

Strong corporate culture and management. A company that possesses core competitiveness and a unique structure allows their top talent to fully demonstrate their ability.

Stability in share ownership and management. Stability in share ownership and management is important. Frequent changes in top management create instability, low morale, and a vicious cycle of decreased efficiency and rashes of departures, through termination or resignation.

Professional ethics

Back to the point of what makes a fund manager stand out, let's not forget that professional ethics ranks high in the equation. A fund manager who lacks professional ethics and uses large sums of clients' money for his or her own interests is basically committing a breach of trust. So-called "rat trading" (see below) is a case in point. The market has been rife with rumors of some fund managers engaging in "rat trading" and complaints filed by listed companies against fund managers who demanded Audi cars as gifts. These are warnings that investors should make sure the managers they entrust their money to are upstanding and professional.

Practical tips

What is "rat trading"?

"Rat trading" refers to the act of bankers (top company executives, key decision makers, relatives, and friends of company honchos) using personal funds to buy shares at low prices to build up stock, before using public funds to push prices higher, and selling personal lots thereafter to take profits. "Rat trading" is a tactic used to switch fortunes, to claim private ownership of public funds. In truth, it is plain corruption and theft.

Stratagem 32

Semblance of Calm in the City (空城计)

The Calm Before the Storm

Origin of the Stratagem

During the Three Kingdoms Period, Zhuge Liang's misplaced trust in military strategist Ma Su caused him to lose Jieting, an important strategic base. Wei General Sima Yi took the opportunity to lead a 150,000-strong army to Xicheng to confront Zhuge Liang, who had no general by his side and just a handful of court officials and 2,500 battalion soldiers. General Sima Yi's imminent attack worried Zhuge Liang's men, but not the shrewd strategist.

As he looked out of the city tower, Zhuge Liang assured his men that he had found a way to get rid of the enemy. He instructed the soldiers to hide all the flags, stay in the city, keep their voices

177

down, open all the four city gates, and have 20 soldiers disguised as common folks washing the grounds above the gates. Zhuge Liang himself donned a red ceremonial robe and tall headgear. With two young pupils and musical instruments in hand, they sat atop the fortress tower burning incense and playing music while watching the enemy's tower at the other end.

Astounded to hear about what was happening in Zhuge Liang's camp, Sima Yi went to the frontline to verify the situation. He was perturbed, and after much pondering, decided to order his frontline and defense forces to swap positions. Sima Yi said: "Zhuge Liang is a cautious person who never takes risks. He must have opened the gates of Jieting with traps set up and waiting for us." Braced with that thought, he proceeded to pull his forces out of the region.

New Spin on Funds

The challenge of receiving up-to-date information
Situations prompt fund companies to withhold information
• Changes in company shareholders
• Changes in fund managers
• Drastic fall in the size of funds

The challenge of receiving up-to-date information

To create "a semblance of calm in the city" is, for all military intents and purposes, to rouse the enemy into greater suspicions. There is also another Chinese saying that "a buyer can never outfox a seller" which underlies one party being privy to more information than the other. Likewise, investors are usually limited in their knowledge and understanding of their fund shareholdings and the fund companies, and any information they get is often delayed. So, investors should keep their eyes peeled toward their funds and the fund companies to prevent them from pulling the rug out from under their feet.

Sensitive information is hard to get hold of, even if investors attend investment seminars or make field trips to the fund companies to investigate, because fund companies, like any financial institutions, are guarded by rigorous information firewall systems. This makes media information releases and news reports all the more essential for investment insights.

Situations prompt fund companies to withhold information

Changes in company shareholders. Fund companies habitually withhold information pending changes in company shareholders. Since the 1990s, shareholder changes in fund companies have not let up largely because every fund company was founded by one or more brokerage or trust company shareholders.

Since 2000, the government has put measures in place to standardize the rules and regulations of the securities market and reform the trust industry. By then, five years of a raging bear stock market had sent many securities and trust firms to the brink of bankruptcy. The eventual fate for some was either foreclosures or mergers and acquisitions.

Soon after that, the Supervisory and Administration Commission introduced a regulation that disallows any individual to sit on the board of more than one fund company. As a result, fund companies scrambled to make sweeping changes in shareholders, sometimes even to the names of the companies. New shareholders proceeded to bring in their own managers, and the impact made by the new blood reverberated through the management system, right to the core of it.

Normally, fund companies with foreign shareholders tend to be relatively more stable in their share ownership structures. However, investors will usually be kept in the dark, sometimes for months, about imminent changes in shareholders or disputes among shareholders, until they are done and dusted. By then, it will be too late to do anything even if investors know that internal discord has disrupted fund performance.

Changes in fund managers. Changes in fund managers have the most direct impact on the performance of funds. It is also an issue that fund companies avoid bringing up.

Reasons for changes in fund managers include:

- Internal transfers: Product innovation and rapid changes in the sizes of funds require companies to make necessary internal adjustments to some job positions.
- Departure of fund managers: Some may leave to join rival fund companies or private equity funds.
- Termination of services: Some fund managers may have performed below par and been asked to leave.

For example, we know of a fund that had a change of three fund managers in four months. Fund companies would rather keep quiet about such changes, especially if they involve celebrity fund managers. Some companies will also quickly promote assistant fund managers or research officers to fill positions left by departing fund managers, or continue to link a celebrity fund manager's name to a fund even after he or she has been transferred to another position internally. There are even former employers who put up public notices of the resignation of some celebrity fund managers two months after these managers had started working for new employers or after earlier news reports about their moves. In such situations, investors can only bank on the media to provide more timely insights and first-hand information than the fund companies.

Drastic fall in the size of funds. Fund companies are also inclined to keep a low profile when the size of their funds falls so much that they teeter on the edge of insolvency. Relentless waves of redemptions may shrink the size of a fund, not only in a bear market but also in a bull market. Small, obscure funds, bond funds yielding lower rates of return, and currency funds are all susceptible to the same problem.

The Measures for the Administration of Operations of Securities Investment stipulates a limit on the number of shareholders allowed in a fund; the number cannot exceed 200. It also rules that the net asset value of a fund must be maintained at RMB50 million or above. Hence, when the size of a fund hangs by a thread, close to the point of insolvency, the fund company will either mobilize its own capital or seek capital injection from relevant agencies for support. Investors are usually unaware of all the goings on until they read the quarterly reports. But how many regular investors who lack professional training or an expert eye will actually pore through those quarterly reports?

At the end of the day, official media reports are sometimes more timely and reliable sources than company notices in helping investors to understand the ins and outs of an investment operation.

Practical tips

China Securities Regulatory Commission's (CSRC) regular information reports on funds have revealed some guidelines, detailing standards on content disclosure and format.

1. **Public notice of fund's net asset value per share.** Every fund has to file the report every day after the securities markets end the day's trading session. The information will be made public the next day. The latest market prices are used to calculate and disclose the fund's net asset market value per share (minus all deficit).

2. **Public notice of quarterly investment portfolios.** The report has to reveal the investment ratio of stocks and bonds in each fund, the industry classification of the stocks, and detailed background information

of the top 10 stocks. The report will be made public within 15 working days after the end of every quarter.

3. **Public notice of half-yearly report.** The report will be made public within 60 days after the first six months of the accounting year have ended to reflect the operation and performance of the fund in the first half of the year. The main contents include the manager's report, a financial analysis of key issues, and so on. The financial analysis report comes with tabulated charts on assets, liabilities, profit, profit distribution, and net asset changes, accounting charts, appendices, and footnotes.

4. **Public notice of annual report.** The report will be made public within 90 days after the accounting year ends to reflect the operation and performance of the fund for the entire year. Besides the provision of contents similar to that of the half-yearly report, the annual report must also include the custodian and auditor's reports.

According to the guidelines, fund companies must also post their bi-yearly and annual verbatim reports on their Web sites, as well as publish key excerpts of the reports in selected newspapers and Web sites, while quarterly reports must be published in full in selected newspapers and Web sites. After the regular public notices are posted, these reports must also be delivered to the homes of fund managers and custodians for their reference and research.

Stratagem 33

The Strategy of Sowing Discord (反间计)

Make Counter Propositions to Reap Extra Profit

Origin of the Stratagem

During the Warring States Period, General Yue Yi of the Yan State fought a long and hard battle with General Tian Dan of the Qi State at Ji Mo. Tian Dan realized that the newly crowned King Yan Huiwang had remained rather suspicious of Yue Yi despite showing a fair amount of trust in him. Tian Dan manipulated the situation by spreading rumors that Yue Yi was planning treason by leaving the Yan State to make himself king of Qi, and had suspended all attacks on Ji Mo in an attempt to win over the Qi masses. Tian Dan also spread rumors that replacing the Yan general would hasten the conquest of Ji Mo. King Yan Huiwang walked right into the trap set up by Tian Dan, and replaced Yue Yi, who saw the tide of change as a threat and fled to the Zhao State. Tian Dan was thus able to decimate the Yan army in one mighty blow.

This story shows how Tian Dan employed the stratagem of "sowing discord" to fuel internal conflicts in the enemy's camp to send it on the road of self-destruction.

New Spin on Funds

The cost issue
Competitive differentials
• Winning service
• Discount opportunities
• Free services

The cost issue

Government policies and regulations usually determine the prices or the rates of charges in financial businesses. For example, central banks set the benchmarks of interest rates for savings and loans, while industry associations propose the benchmarks for different types of securities commissions. Likewise, fund companies may hail from different regions and backgrounds, but the charges for similar fund products are almost the same. The management fee of a share-based fund is normally set at 1.5 percent; the application and subscription fees are usually set at 1.2 percent and 1.5 percent respectively, adjustable according to the level of capital investment; and the redemption fee is fixed at 0.5 percent. In the case of a bond fund, the management fee is 0.8 percent, while a currency fund charges a management fee of 0.33 percent. The list goes on.

This may make investors wonder why they have to pay the same rates for products that come in a multitude of qualities in a highly competitive fund market, or pay almost the same rates for two products that sit on different ends of the spectrum. The reason is, the fees and prices do not have built-in self-adjustment capabilities to enable them to respond to market forces of supply and demand accordingly, unlike the prices of meat, poultry, eggs, and vegetables, or the prices of electrical products that fluctuate in tandem with production cycles.

Competitive differentials

Costs alone do not tell investors much about the quality of one product over another, or help investors to identify suitable products to buy. But looking at the past performance results, the rankings, and the current core competitiveness of funds may give investors some clues. Competition has also created differentials in quality and brand.

The same can be said of the charges of fund companies. They may appear to be set in stone, but if you study them carefully you will notice how market competition has given rise to differentials in service, sales promotion methods, discount channels, purchase methods, and so on. Through these differentials, investors may pick up bargains and lucrative deals.

Winning service. On one hand, statistical data indicates that more than 50 percent of fund investors buy fund products through banks, because banks are closer to home, and are more convenient in terms of networks. On the other hand, fund companies offer investors multiple ways to make their purchases, through direct sales centers and one-on-one professional services provided by customer managers to direct sales customers. These professional services include the use of point of sale (POS) cards to make fund purchases, to save customers the hassle of having to carry huge amounts of cash and checkbooks. Customer managers, armed with mobile POS machines, will even make door-to-door visits to serve premium customers, to enable them to open accounts on the spot, and to offer advice on the markets. Such advice is usually more professional and reliable than the service provided by the sales agents. Customers can also call the customer managers directly instead of calling the customer service center and being put on hold or made to wait in line.

Discount opportunities. Most fund companies offer online electronic trading. To encourage customers to use it, many fund companies give discounts on subscription fees, which may not be offered by sales agents. The discounts vary from company to company, and from period to period in sales promotion. Some offer discounts of 20 percent, so the fees may drop to as low as 0.8 percent or 0.6 percent. It is no small amount in savings if you are investing a huge sum of money, or if you add up the discounts for various fees.

Some funds split up subscription fees into front-end and back-end charges. An investor is only required to pay a back-end fee upon the redemption of a fund. Once an investor has held the fund for a stipulated period, the back-end fee will be progressively discounted, or eventually waived. Funds that are held for more than three to five years normally have a zero subscription charge rate, as fund companies seek to encourage investors to hold funds over a long period. Hence, investors who have no intention to redeem their funds within a short period should opt for back-end payments. Bank officers may not inform investors of the option sometimes, because as sales agents, they have no reason to delay or give up the revenue that they can make on the spot.

Of course, it is possible to enjoy discount privileges by buying funds from banks; that is, if you do so through fixed investment. Once you have made fixed investments a certain number of times, you will be able to apply for subscription at a discount. Chances are, you will find many sales agents running similar policies, and investors should capitalize on them. Take, for example, the subscription fee for a fixed investment made after 12 investments that will enjoy a discounted rate of as low as 0.6 percent. What you should do is utilize a small pool of capital for the first 12 fixed investments before beefing up the amount to take advantage of the huge discount on the subscription fee. All in all, it will lower your costs by a large margin.

Free services. Fund companies also offer a plethora of free services, such as SMS updates on funds and markets, as well as free mail delivery of invoices and investment publications. Just open your eyes to the details on the Web or ask the customer managers, and you will be able to subscribe to these publications. As the market develops, companies will launch even more discounts and value-added services to attract investors. Investors should always look out for the competitive differentials of the fund companies to take advantage of the ones that offer the most discounts and privileges.

Stratagem 34

Inflict Harm on Oneself to Gain Sympathy (苦肉计)

True Lies

Origin of the Stratagem

During the Three Kingdoms Period, Cao Cao had a million troops stationed in Chibi in a strong line of defense. No matter how hard Liu Bei's allied forces tried to break it, their efforts always came up short. Subsequently, veteran general Huang Gai got the go-ahead from Governor Zhou Yu to stage a fire attack. However, no one would lay the groundwork for the attack against Cao Cao's massive warships. When Huang Gai heard the news, he volunteered to execute the plan. Zhou Yu reacted by saying: "How can we convince Cao Cao without making some sacrifices?" and Huang Gai replied: "I owe the king my gratitude, and I shall sacrifice my life for him without regrets."

The next day, Zhou Yu met with the generals to discuss their war strategy. Every general was told to store up three months of grain supplies in preparation for combat. Unexpectedly, Huang Gai started singing a different tune, much to Zhou Yu's annoyance. He then ordered his henchmen to take Huang Gai out to be executed. Only persistent pleas from the other men swayed Zhou Yu to spare his life. Nevertheless, Huang Gai still had to suffer 50 strokes of the cane. Every witness was reduced to tears when they saw Huang Gai flogged to a pulp. His flesh was raw and bloody, and he nearly passed out a few times.

At long last, Huang Gai's strategy of "inflicting harm on himself to gain sympathy" paid off. In the middle of one night, he decided it was time to set sail with more than 20 warships toward the enemy vessels. Huang Gai knew the enemy troops' guard would be down when they saw him coming with flags raised in surrender. He then took them by surprise by launching a fire attack. Despite being weaker in numbers, Huang Gai's troops overpowered Cao Cao's formidable force.

New Spin on Funds

Temporary halt in subscription
- Oversubscription
- Major asset restructuring and share allocation reform
- Large blocks of dividend payout
- Unfavorable market conditions

Temporary halt in subscription

Stratagem 9 touches on the topic of taking a wait-and-see attitude toward the closed period of new funds. It is not uncommon also for old funds to halt subscription or redemption on a temporary basis. With markets becoming more capricious, and more new elements coming into play, funds are shuttling between open and closed periods even more frequently. It can create a big headache or be a dilemma for investors, as the closed periods forbid any buying or selling.

Instead of begrudging the system, investors may want to ask why funds need to call for a temporary halt in subscription and redemption. Suspending subscription stops the flow of capital into a fund, which will retard its growth in size. The fund company will also take a hit in income as the management fee is based on a percentage of the market value of the fund. This is also the only source of income for the fund company after the initial subscription charges.

There is an ancient Chinese saying that "nobody would do harm to oneself, but if inflicted, the harm must be real." Knowing men's tendency to think in this manner, Zhou Yu flogged his general Huang Gai, to put the stratagem "inflicting harm on oneself to gain sympathy" to work.

Calling a halt to the subscription of a fund hurts business, but a fund must surely have a good reason for doing so. The fund may be putting its size and income on hold in exchange for a more stable net asset value and the trust of its investors.

Oversubscription. Oversubscription may cause the size of a fund to expand too much, and thus the need to halt subscription temporarily. An overpriced fund in the stock market is hard for a fund manager to sell and operate. That, in turn, will put a dent in the fund's investment return. Hence, it is necessary for fund companies to control the size of funds, especially high-profile and branded funds. Investors tend to shun funds that are considered large in size, as they will undermine investment efficiency.

Major asset restructuring and share allocation reform. Massive asset restructuring and share allocation reform are likely to have a huge impact on the net asset value of a fund. Thus, a temporary halt in subscription in the course of such events will prevent massive speculative profit-taking from draining a fund of capital or hurting the profit margins of genuine investors. That said, few funds impose a closed period in the midst of a major asset restructuring or share allocation reform. Most funds allow free capital inflows and outflows.

Large blocks of dividend payout. When a fund company is preparing to hand out dividends, it will impose a closed period to prevent a large influx of capital from destabilizing the stockholding ratio of the fund. However, it is not uncommon for funds to flag massive dividend payouts to attract more investment capital to beef up the size of their funds.

Unfavorable market conditions. In other cases, subscription is suspended due to considerations given to higher market estimates, investor interest, and combined risk evaluation, and it could have stemmed from a fund manager's poor after-market forecast, or some other reasons.

Some funds may halt subscription for as long as six months, or even longer. A small-sized fund is easy to operate, and tends to rank relatively high in net asset growth. Investors barred from subscribing to one fund may still be drawn toward funds of similar brands and types under the same company. Some funds may debut as close-end funds but be open for subscription a few days later, although redemption may not be permitted to spur a rapid increase in the size of the funds. These are tactics that investors should keep an eye out for.

Stratagem 35

The Strategy of Combined Tactics
(连环计)

Mix Strategies to Fortify Funds

Origin of the Stratagem

The strategy of using combined tactics means having tactics interlinked and running concurrently to create an invincible shield against attack. Song General Bi Zaiyu once employed the strategy to secure an impressive win.

He started with guerilla warfare that required a high degree of mobility in attack and defense. Jin soldiers were visibly worn out after being forced to move back and forth, as well as start and stop their tactical moves. When they stumbled onto the heavily flavored cooked black beans that Bi Zaiyu had scattered all over the battleground, they wolfed them down to sooth famished stomachs and parched throats. After that, the soldiers would not budge or advance from the position, leaving the Jin army in paralysis and total disarray in the middle of the night. Bi Zaiyu quickly mobilized all units to close in on the enemy, before a massacre of the Jin army seriously began.

New Spin on Funds

Multi-pronged investment strategy
A pyramid approach
Points to consider
Guidelines to portfolio adjustments
Regular checks and updates

Multi-pronged investment strategy

Making an investment tests a person's courage, shrewdness, and judgment. For the uninitiated, making the decision to invest in funds is only the beginning. Questions such as the types of funds to buy, the fund companies to sign up with, and the redemption period can be mind-boggling. They require lots of legwork and a thorough assessment.

Fund portfolios enable investors to spread out risk to an optimal level, and enjoy professional financial consultation. A fund portfolio is the allotment of one's assets into several funds, and a combination of strategies is needed to create a successful portfolio. It is not simply a matter of putting two funds together.

A pyramid approach

First, let's look at how we can approach our investment by way of a pyramid:

- Set investment goals.
- Draft an investment plan.
- Allot assets to shares and fixed yields.

- Divide the investment markets (after the inception of QDII).
- Classify the various types of funds.
- Choose funds.

The pyramid approach is show in Figure 35.1.

From setting investment goals and analyzing those targets, to determining asset allocation and the different classification of funds, the top-down approach will produce a plausible portfolio. Let's say your investment aim is to amass US$2 million in assets over a 30-year period. That means you will have to make a US$1,000 investment every month, and expect a 10 percent return rate to achieve your investment target after a 30-year period.

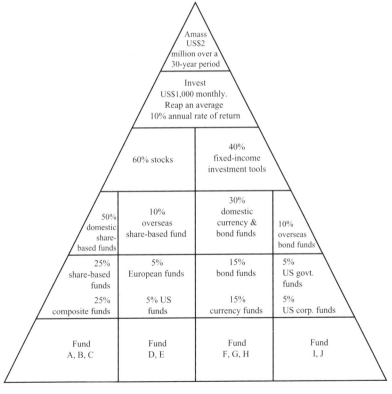

Figure 35.1 Pyramid Approach

Asset allocation shapes an investment portfolio. It also represents the ratio of different types of funds held, which are very much predetermined by an investor's age, investment goals, appetite for risk, and so on. The ratio of share-based funds in an older investor's portfolio should be lower compared to that of a young investor.

Points to consider

- Different types of funds vary in terms of returns, security, and liquidity. They complement one another in a fund portfolio.
- It is important that your fund portfolio satisfies your risk/return preference. A fund may affect the risk/return level of the portfolio, but not in its entirety.
- Younger investors may have asset portfolios that include share-based funds.
- Older investors may have asset portfolios that contain fixed-income funds.

You have built your portfolio, but that is not the end of the story. Check the performance of your portfolio regularly to see if it meets your expectations.

Guidelines to portfolio adjustments

Generally speaking, there are three guidelines to making portfolio adjustments:

- Fund performance: Remove a fund that is underperforming.
- Changes in funds: This may involve changes in fund managers or adjustments made to investment strategies.
- Investment period: If the investment period is cut short, it is time to reduce the ratio of high-risk funds in the portfolio.

Regular checks and updates

There is no need for an investor to check on the returns of his or her portfolio day in, day out, but a check every six months is necessary. Stay focused once you have taken the first step to construct the pyramid, and stick by what you have set out to achieve. You will see your assets grow robustly as anticipated, just like the pleasure parents take in watching their sons and daughters blossom.

Practical tips

Proposed portfolios from investors of different profiles

Investor profile	Proposed portfolios
Conservative	80 percent bond fund/currency fund, 20 percent share-based fund
Balanced	40 percent bond fund/currency fund, 60 percent share-based fund
Active	20 percent bond fund/currency fund, 80 percent share-based fund

Stratagem 36

If All Else Fails, Beat a Retreat
(走为上计)

Overseas Investment as the Best Bet

Origin of the Stratagem

During the Warring States Period, King Chu Zhuangwang of Chu met fierce resistance from the Yong State when he tried to annex the smaller state in a bid to extend his power base. Chu General Shi Shu then advised the king to feign defeat to fool the Yong soldiers into complacency. The plan was immediately put into motion. The Chu troops let the Yong soldiers win seven battles in succession. Victory soon went to their heads, and made them let down their guard against the Chu forces. King Chu Zhuangwang knew the time was ripe for his troops to move in on the Yong State from two sides. Still flushed with victory, the Yong warriors never expected the Chu army to stage a retaliation so soon. Caught off-guard, they could only fight a haphazard war that sounded the death knell of the Yong State.

New Spin on Funds

The QDII window to the world
Reasons to invest in QDII funds
Types of QDII funds

The QDII window to the world

QDII is a window to the outside world that is finally open to Chinese investors after years of waiting. No matter how rosy the development and prospects of the A-share market are, overseas markets will always provide Chinese investors with a broader set of options to spread out risk, build more balanced portfolios, and achieve their financial goals in a steadier and more stable fashion. Therefore, moving from the A-share market to the overseas markets is a step up in strategy.

Reasons to invest in QDII funds

- **Even small amounts of cash work**
  Any direct buying and selling in overseas stocks usually involves a staggering amount of money. Hong Kong blue chip and market heavyweight HSBC (stock code: 0005) is trading at around US$18 at the time of writing. A purchase of 400 shares will require US$7,300. Through QDII funds, you could purchase them for as low as US$143 to achieve your dream of investing overseas.

- **No fuss in registration, relatively low costs**
  Investors are required to pay transaction fees and currency conversion fees for all direct investment in Hong Kong stocks. But those fees are waived for overseas investment made through

QDII funds. As the size of QDII funds is exceptionally large, they usually offer a variety of discounts in handling and custodial charges for stock investment from overseas. The costs and time taken for paperwork are also drastically reduced, compared to direct investment.

- **Professionals rule the roost**
  There is still a dearth of information on overseas markets in China. However, a QDII fund specialist in charge of investment strategy is supported by an information network with global coverage. From there, the fund specialist is able to gather relevant statistics and information for investors, to keep them informed of market activity, and to enable them to boost their investment profit.

Types of QDII funds

Regardless of the types of QDII funds you are looking to buy, first and foremost find out the investors they are targeting, their investment scope, and their risk profile. The ratio of shares, bonds, cash, and so on differ from one QDII fund to another. The asset allocation ratio by country or regional market is also variable. Just to cite a few examples, you have the developed markets versus the emerging markets, or publicly listed companies that hail from different overseas stock exchanges. If you have a product invested in overseas funds, study the features of those funds, how the fund managers put together a basket of products, the indices against which the performance of funds is benchmarked, and the index weightings. That will shed more light on the investment style of the fund.

Also find out whether the fund companies, managers, and overseas investment advisors enjoy a good reputation, uphold creditable brands, and come with rich overseas investment experience.

It never hurts to be cost-conscious as well. Find out what the lowest rates are for application, subscription, redemption, and custodial. They tend to be very different to domestic open-end funds. A final reminder: always determine the currencies used for pricing.

Practical tips

QDII funds versus Hong Kong funds

QDII funds are vastly different from funds such as ETFs (exchange traded funds) and REITs (real estate investment trusts) which are listed and traded on the Hong Kong Stock Exchange (HKSE).

There are more than a dozen ETFs being traded on the HKSE, and many of them also track the global and Asia-Pacific markets, such as India, South Korea, and the US. Apart from ETFs linked to stock markets, some ETFs are linked to bonds, commercial products, and so on. Are these funds more attractive than QDII funds? There is no definite answer. It very much depends on which angle you take.

To invest overseas, one must not only have a good grasp of the global markets, but also keep a sharp eye on the movements of foreign exchange rates as they make a huge impact on profits. The Hong Kong dollar is pegged to the US dollar while the *renminbi* continues to appreciate against the US dollar. For that reason alone, it is essential for any investor to weigh in on the foreign exchange risks of buying funds quoted in Hong Kong dollars and US dollars.

Current developments show that QDII funds issued in China provide quicker and timelier after-sale service, as well as more informative strategic reports, market research, and other data. Hence, investors spend less time and money communicating. However, they encounter a "gap" in terms of trying to obtain fund services abroad. Language is a barrier; the majority of overseas funds provide information in English.

Of course, that should not be an investor's uppermost consideration in selecting a fund. The key is to determine whether a fund investment strategy can capitalize on market trends, and whether its operations and performance are stable and strong in the medium and long term. It is a point that applies to fund investment anywhere in the world.

Index